60 Delicious Gluten-Free Plant-Based Recipes

Earthy VEGAN EATS

Maria Gureeva

Founder of
EARTH OF MARIA

First published in 2021 by
Page Street Publishing Co.
27 Congress Street, Suite 105
Salem, MA 01970
www.pagestreetpublishing.com

Distributed by Macmillan, sales in Canada by The Canadian Manda Group.

25 24 23 22 21 1 2 3 4 5

ISBN-13: 978-1-64567-267-8
ISBN-10: 1-64567-267-0

Library of Congress Control Number: 2020942239

Cover and book design by Rosie Stewart for Page Street Publishing Co.
Photography by Maria Gureeva

Printed and bound in China

Page Street Publishing protects our planet by donating to nonprofits like The Trustees, which focuses on local land conservation.

TO MY MUM, DAD AND EVERYONE
WHO HAS SUPPORTED ME THROUGHOUT MY JOURNEY
TO BECOME A BETTER ME.

Contents

My Vegan Journey

Hi, everyone! Thank you so much for being here, reading this book. I hope you get a huge amount of value out of it and that the recipes you make brighten your day. Before we jump into the food, I want to quickly share how I came to this point in my journey with food and veganism, and also explain the core values of my first cookbook.

Where do I start? Looking back, my health journey had countless phases and even numerous starting points given the number of times I slipped up and had to return to square one. But for us to get to know each other, I'll try to tell the story of what led to me writing *Earthy Vegan Eats* as linearly as possible, explaining along the way my reasoning for adopting a healthy vegan diet.

I was born in a mid-sized Russian town on an unusually cold afternoon in May. Growing up in a family of foodies with large appetites, I learned to love cooking from scratch at an early age with the help of my mum and grandma. Even before I entered formal education, they equipped me with fundamental life skills—often when I would have preferred to spend my afternoons playing outside or mindlessly watching cartoons. But looking back, I know that without my family's influence I may not have developed my creative energy later in life.

Now, if you ever visit Russia, you'll instantly recognize the importance of food to Russian culture. My childhood was no different. And while many Russian dishes are heavy in animal products, my family chose a diet centered on whole foods that came straight from the earth. In 2008, my mum and I left our entire lives behind and moved to the U.K. An astronomical change in cuisine awaited us, but we stuck as closely as possible to our old ways of eating: lots of fruits and vegetables, cooking everything ourselves, limiting restaurants and takeout to a few times a month.

My first obstacle came in my early teenage years, when I developed unhealthy restrictive eating habits and was quickly diagnosed with anorexia nervosa. Eating disorders are incredibly complicated and difficult to attribute to a single cause; I, after all, had a great relationship with food until that point, did not limit my calorie intake and stayed in shape easily through exercise. But my anxiety from school, perfectionism and a self-critical nature came together to push me over the edge; I gradually lost my carefree attitude toward food and my body.

I'm glad to see that more people are recognizing that eating disorders are never as simple as just wanting to be skinny. Their complexity is exactly what makes treatment so difficult. Often, as in my case, the affected individual has to recognize that the life that lies beyond their unhealthy habits and routines is much, much happier.

I was in a relapse when I first came across veganism. At first cutting out all animal products from one's diet and life seemed radical to me, as it did to most people half a decade ago. But it didn't take a lot of research to understand why more people were switching over to a plant-based lifestyle, and why it resonated so strongly with my own core values.

I knew a little bit about where our food came from, but researching the vegan movement opened my eyes to the detrimental impact of animal agriculture on our planet and the lives of animals. It's the ethical component of veganism which had the most profound impact on me. I could no longer look at animal products in the same way, and I felt an urge to transform my whole lifestyle overnight. At the same time, I couldn't simply ignore what I was going through personally, and I used veganism as a way to reclaim my life, gain weight and change my attitude toward food.

Taking this plunge into seeing food in an entirely different way, I recovered with far fewer setbacks than I expected. With our final school exams around the corner, I knew I needed to eat and challenge myself to cut back my excessive exercise to get the grades I wanted and increase my chances of getting into my dream university, the University of Oxford.

I finally went vegan in September 2015, and I have never doubted my decision. Given my inherent love for wholesome plant-based food, I found the transition easy. Furthermore, it revived my love for food. My mum and I take an annual trip to visit our family, and when one of my best friends joined our two-week trip in 2017, the five-course meals served up to us by each household we visited surprised her, and resulted in an embarrassing number of food comas for both of us. Thankfully, everyone was fascinated with, rather than confused by, my new way of eating.

Veganism does require a lot of commitment and research. You have to be vigilant about hidden animal products and—given the lower calorie density of a lot of vegan food—you need to eat enough to sustain your lifestyle. For this to be a long-term lifestyle, it's also important to supplement certain vitamins and minerals, such as B12. But these days, veganism feels like an inherent part of who I am and I will forever be grateful for how it changed me and my life for the better.

Behind The Lens:

HOW I STARTED EARTH OF MARIA

My upbringing had a strong influence on my journey with food and my transition to veganism. Veganism also helped me to discover my passions and skills, and I found a community which helped me grow not just in terms of my career, but also as a person.

I launched the Earth of Maria Instagram account in the summer of 2017 as a side project with zero expectations, just to test the waters a little bit and see what the whole social media thing was about. I enjoyed browsing Instagram to gather inspiration for my own cooking and quickly acquainted myself with vegan cuisine through the work of countless talented chefs. I developed my own recipes and took photos using an old DSLR camera, posting them online on a casual schedule during my pre-university gap year. I grew a small community of a few thousand, and in 2018, I got much more serious about growing my social media and also launching my website packed full of my favorite recipes.

After massively expanding my cooking skills and getting a taste of an online presence, I poured more effort into the other facets of blogging: search engine optimization, better recipe writing and photography—which is now my favorite creative outlet. Around this time, I also switched to a predominantly gluten-free diet. I had experienced symptoms of gluten intolerance, and when I developed recipes that were both plant-based and gluten-free, I received a lot of positive feedback from people who couldn't eat gluten for medical reasons.

I've grown my community a lot and made lifelong friends along the way. We all support each other and share the same passion for making the world a better place through the power of food. There's so much room for innovation in the online recipe space, in the food industry and in the world. And I'm beyond grateful to be a part of it, using my voice to help people live a balanced, healthy lifestyle and eat more plants one meal at a time.

About This Book

The main theme of this book? Creative, vibrant and healthy vegan comfort food. As I developed these recipes, I challenged myself to add twists to old favorites and try out new combinations. After all, plain porridge for breakfast quickly gets boring. I wanted to explore a multitude of cooking techniques while keeping things approachable for anyone—from an experienced plant-based chef to a complete beginner in the kitchen.

My ideal dish is characterized by a unique depth of texture and flavor, using a combination of simple ingredients to create something that makes you feel a higher level of contentment. But *Earthy Vegan Eats* is also all about balance. An earthy meal can be a vibrant and hearty salad bursting with fresh vegetables, followed by a slice of your favorite dessert, each forkful of which is much more enjoyable because you made it from scratch. I love using plenty of spices and natural ingredients to create unique flavors.

With just a few tricks, anyone can prepare restaurant-quality food from the comfort of their own kitchen. I love simple recipes, but my passion for vegan food comes down to its versatility and how it can tell a story through how it looks and tastes.

In this book you will find 60 recipes that are entirely vegan and gluten-free and taste delicious every time. Many are ideal for feeding a family or even just yourself. Others make a great addition to party tables whenever you're keen to impress friends or family with the culinary potential of plants. The book emphasizes cooking from scratch, whether it's a pizza base, a pie crust or a vegan alternative to ingredients such as honey and cheese. I provide helpful tips along the way to make the cooking process easier and much more enjoyable. And if you come across an unfamiliar ingredient or technique, I encourage you to try it out, because you might discover a new favorite!

Top Ten Tips to Cook Gourmet Gluten-Free Vegan Food—

EVEN AS A BEGINNER!

Whether you want to go vegan, eat a predominantly plant-based diet or simply sprinkle in a vegan dish here and there, knowing how to cook an incredible meal or bake a dessert from scratch with no animal products will make the transition a lot easier. This applies even more if you follow a gluten-free diet. Before we jump into the recipes, here are my top ten cooking tips that will change every plant-based home cook's life!

1. SPICES ARE EVERYTHING.

I can't say this enough. Spices make your food much tastier—and healthier, too! Always use more than you think you need: I used to make the mistake of adding less than ¼ teaspoon of cumin and just a little bit of salt to my tofu scramble, and I wondered why it turned out bland. Try different combinations, gaining inspiration from different cultures and culinary traditions. Chances are you'll be amazed by how much you can create using spices you probably have in your cupboard already. My personal favorites are cumin, turmeric, garam masala, garlic powder and smoked paprika; I use them daily.

2. CASHEWS ARE YOUR BEST FRIEND.

Worried that by cooking vegan food, you'll have to let go of your favorite creamy sauces? Don't panic, because cashews are here for you. Soaking and blending cashews allows you to make creamy salad dressings, sauces and even various desserts that are known for their silky-smooth quality! The trick here is to invest in a good-quality high-speed blender or food processor. This will ensure that your blended cashews have no leftover chunks and a smooth, as opposed to a grainy, texture. Soak them for at least four hours—but no more than eight—or boil them in a saucepan for 15 minutes. I'd recommend using the latter technique with a high-speed blender; otherwise, stick to the former. A properly soaked cashew will fall apart when you squeeze it between your fingers.

3. LEARN HOW TO COOK VEGETABLES.

My favorite way to create complex, interesting flavors is knowing how to cook vegetables in many ways! They are undoubtedly good for you, and they also carry a lot of natural flavor that comes out during the cooking process and varies depending on the cooking technique you choose. That's why I make sure that each one of my savory meals contains at least a handful of servings. Whether you sauté, bake, roast or simply add them to your meal, raw vegetables will add color and make your cooking a lot more interesting.

Also, don't be afraid to cook vegetables for a while! For instance, I see many people sautéing garlic and onion for a few seconds before adding the rest of the ingredients. Give them a few minutes in the frying pan to deepen the flavors—and you'll see how a simple change to how you cook can make a huge difference to the final result!

4. SALT BELONGS IN EVERYTHING!

In these recipes, I include suggested amounts of salt. Taste as you go and adjust the amount depending on your preference. Of course, don't go overboard: too much salt isn't great for your health, and it will overpower the overall flavor profile of the dish. But salt added a little bit at a time to achieve a perfect balance is probably the simplest guaranteed method for making better food. And don't be afraid of salt in sweet treats. Salted caramel is a classic combination for a reason! Your sweet treats will still be sweet, but with an extra wow-factor.

5. A GOOD SAUCE MAKES EVERYTHING BETTER.

Learn how to make staple sauces and flavorful salad dressings and you're good to go. For instance, a sweet-and-sour sauce can be added to anything from chickpeas to tofu and tempeh. Creamy sauces are perfect for pastas, salads and stirring into soups at the last minute. Salad dressings with the right balance between acidity and sweetness will turn a boring salad into a culinary masterpiece.

6. UNDERSTAND HOW DIFFERENT FLOURS BEHAVE.

Flours are the key to gluten-free cooking and baking. And it's what makes gluten-free cuisine much more interesting—almost like an intellectual challenge! There are countless gluten-free flours out there, but these are some of my favorites. I encourage you to experiment rather than always sticking to store-bought blends.

Chickpea flour: It's light, airy and achieves an exceptional rise. I love using it in foods such as pancakes, muffins and various breads. Remember that chickpea flour does have a distinctive flavor; if you don't enjoy it, you can easily mask it by combining it with other flours and baking/cooking for long enough. Keep in mind, the flavor does cook off to an extent. It's much more subtle after cooking/baking.

Rice flour: Now, there are different types of rice flour. White rice flour is much lighter than brown rice flour, and therefore achieves a better rise. Brown rice flour is much better for breads and baked goods that strive for a denser texture. Be aware that poor-quality rice flour can have a bit of a gritty texture. This will be very apparent and, to make matters worse, the flour won't combine well with the other ingredients.

Buckwheat flour: Buckwheat flour is dense and heavy, packed full of nutrients, and it has a strong, earthy flavor. It works best in breads and other savory recipes, particularly if paired with other flours to complement its qualities.

Coconut flour: Coconut flour is higher in fat, lower in carbs, heavy and very absorbent. Thus, you want to use it with plenty of liquid and in small quantities to start with. It does taste and smell like coconut on its own, which can be great if that's the flavor profile you're going for. You can combine it with other flours for a more neutral flavor, without losing the creamy and smooth texture it creates.

Oat flour: This is another light and fluffy flour that achieves great results. Oat flour is deep, without being super overpowering. In my experience, this is one of the most versatile flours, perfect for anything from pancakes to cookies and cake sponges.

Almond flour: This is not simply ground almonds. It delivers a much finer texture and is more comparable to actual flour than finely ground nuts. It has a very pleasant, natural, almost custardy flavor. Almond flour is an excellent option if you want a moist texture: chewy cookies, flourless cakes and biscuits that melt in your mouth. It's also great for baking that's both vegan and Paleo!

7. PREPARE YOUR INGREDIENTS IN ADVANCE.

Pretty much any experienced cook sticks by this rule. It's the easiest way to reduce overwhelm in the kitchen and save a lot of time. Prepping ahead also allows you to make recipes with greater accuracy by getting the timing correct—instead of scrambling to find the right ingredient just as the rest of the food is about to burn!

8. VEGANIZE YOUR FAVORITES!

If you don't know what to make for special occasions or even for dinner on your own, look at the dishes you enjoy eating, or ones that you loved before you went vegan or switched to a more plant-based way of eating. If you're feeding a crowd, think about what usually captures everyone's attention and ends in praise for the cook—and re-create that, but with all plant-based ingredients. Use flax eggs instead of eggs, plant-based milk instead of dairy milk, coconut oil or peanut butter instead of normal butter, textured vegetable protein (TVP) in place of meat, etc. Once you do this enough, it'll slowly become easier to recognize what works and what doesn't, and you'll see your cooking skills skyrocket.

9. COOK FROM SCRATCH.

Now, I know that most of us live incredibly busy lives. On days not specifically dedicated to recipe testing, I just don't have time to make vegan cheese or fresh pizza dough. But making the basics, such as vegan cheese, chocolate and various breads, is incredibly satisfying, healthier, gives you full control over the ingredients, and it's less expensive, too!

10. ALWAYS CONTINUE LEARNING.

This is the number one thing that I've discovered during my cooking journey: the potential for learning and improvement is truly infinite. There are always new ingredients to discover, new flavor combinations and techniques to learn, new ways to reinvent your old favorites. At first, failing in the kitchen feels discouraging. You think you're hopeless at cooking and will have to stick to restaurants, microwave meals and very basic recipes, such as porridge and avocado toast. That can be accentuated when starting a plant-based way of eating, because you're suddenly overwhelmed by countless new ingredients.

But the trick is to keep trying and take small steps forward. Set goals for yourself: Try one new ingredient each week and cook from blogs or a cookbook three times a week. Watch educational videos on YouTube and listen to cooking podcasts; they taught me things about the art of cooking that I apply on a daily basis. Most importantly, keep it fun and lighthearted, choosing recipes you enjoy and that come naturally to you.

Breakfast in Bed

Start your day right with a luxurious breakfast or brunch. These recipes are bursting with flavor and wholesome ingredients, which is precisely what defines an earthy meal. Skip restaurants and invite your friends over for a homemade brunch that everyone will love, regardless of dietary preference.

This chapter is full of sweet and savory options. Try a simple oatmeal with a unique twist (page 34) or enjoy a vibrant, elegant meal packed full of vegetables that makes you feel like you're having your first meal of the day at a five-star hotel. Whether you want to learn how to make vegan sausages at home (page 22) or reinvent chia pudding (page 18), my selection of breakfast recipes has you covered.

Cheesy Skillet Potatoes and Asparagus

MAKES 4 SERVINGS

1 tbsp (15 ml) olive oil

1 medium onion, chopped

1 clove garlic, minced

½ cup (35 g) chopped mushrooms

25 oz (709 g) white starchy potatoes, chopped into bite-sized chunks (Russets are perfect for this recipe)

1 tsp ground cumin

1 cup (240 ml) plant-based milk

1 tsp ground turmeric

¼ cup (32 g) nutritional yeast

2 tbsp (30 ml) tamari

5 oz (142 g) asparagus, chopped

Chopped tomatoes, for garnish (optional)

Chopped parsley, for garnish (optional)

Savory breakfasts can help set the tone for a slow, luxurious weekend. If you want to impress friends and family, do something a bit more special than just avocado toast or baked beans. These skillet potatoes crisp up perfectly and taste exceptional combined with a rich, dairy-free cheese sauce.

Heat the olive oil in a large nonstick frying pan over medium-high heat. Add the onion and the garlic. Sauté for 2 to 3 minutes, until softened and fragrant. Add the mushrooms and cook for 2 to 3 minutes, until they begin to soften. Add the potatoes, ¼ cup (60 ml) of water and the cumin. Stir to combine, then cook over medium heat for around 15 minutes, stirring frequently, to allow the potatoes to soften.

Add the plant-based milk, turmeric, nutritional yeast and tamari. Stir well and continue to simmer for 10 minutes, until the potatoes are fully cooked through and tender.

Stir in the asparagus and continue cooking for 5 minutes, until the asparagus is bright green and soft. Serve immediately. Garnish with tomatoes and parsley, if using.

NOTE: You can add any other veggies of your choice to customize this dish. Sweet potatoes work really well, too.

Earl Grey Chia Pudding

MAKES 1 SERVING

PUDDING

½ cup (120 ml) vegan yogurt

½ cup (120 ml) plant-based milk

2 tbsp (20 g) chia seeds

1 large banana, mashed

1 tbsp (15 ml) maple syrup

1 Earl Grey tea bag

TOPPINGS

½ cup (83 g) chopped fresh strawberries

½ large banana, chopped

1 tbsp (15 g) tahini

Mixed nuts

Chopped dark chocolate

Chia pudding is a classic vegan breakfast that's great for eating on the go. It's simple, but there are countless flavor combinations to try out to make sure it never gets boring. Earl Grey is one of my favorites, adding a layer of luxury to the base and a unique flavor that will make breakfast much more enjoyable. Serve this with tangy, sweet strawberries on top to enhance the sophistication of the pudding—and make it a perfect dessert, too.

In a large mixing bowl, whisk together the vegan yogurt, plant-based milk, chia seeds, mashed banana, maple syrup and the contents of the Earl Grey tea bag.

Transfer the mixture to a jar or a small bowl. Leave it in the fridge for at least 30 minutes, preferably overnight.

Serve with the strawberries, banana, tahini, mixed nuts and dark chocolate.

Simple Waffles

MAKES 10 TO 12 WAFFLES

- ¼ cup (42 g) ground flaxseed
- 1½ cups (240 g) rice flour
- 1 cup (120 g) tapioca flour
- 1 cup (124 g) corn flour
- 2 tsp (6 g) xanthan gum
- ⅓ cup (48 g) coconut sugar
- 1 tsp salt
- 3 cups (720 ml) plant-based milk
- ¼ cup (60 ml) apple cider vinegar
- ½ cup (110 g) coconut oil, melted
- 2 tsp (10 ml) vanilla extract
- Cooking spray

What I love about waffles is just how versatile they are. You can serve them with fruit, maple syrup, nut butter or any other toppings of your choice. If you have some left over, simply freeze them and reheat for breakfast or a quick snack at any point in the day. This is my go-to waffle recipe. Expect crunchiness on the outside, a soft and fluffy center and just the right amount of sweetness!

Make the flax egg by combining the ground flaxseed and ½ cup (120 ml) of water. Set aside to soak for around 10 minutes.

In a large mixing bowl, combine the rice flour, tapioca flour, corn flour, xanthan gum, coconut sugar and salt. In a separate mixing bowl, combine the plant-based milk, flax egg, apple cider vinegar, coconut oil and vanilla. Add the wet ingredients to the dry and mix until well combined.

Spray your waffle maker with cooking spray and preheat it according to the manufacturer's instructions. When it is hot, transfer around ⅓ to ½ cup (80 to 120 ml) of the batter to the center of the waffle plate. Close the waffle maker and cook each waffle for 5 to 7 minutes, until crispy and golden brown.

Homemade Vegan Sausages

MAKES 6 SAUSAGES

1½ tbsp (23 ml) olive oil, divided

⅔ cup (106 g) finely chopped onion

2 cups (140 g) sliced baby bella mushrooms

1 (15-oz [425-g]) can white beans or butter beans, drained and rinsed

1 tbsp (16 g) tomato paste

1 tsp salt

¼ cup (15 g) finely chopped fresh parsley

1 tbsp (15 ml) lemon juice

½ tsp black pepper

¾ cup (69 g) chickpea flour

Vegan meat alternatives are increasingly available at any grocery store, but it's easy to make them at home, keeping them healthy and full of flavor. You need just over half an hour to make these sausages from scratch—perfect for a slow weekend brunch with no hassle! Serve them on toast or with vegetables and a dipping sauce of your choice. You can even add them to a vegan roast dinner (page 44).

If baking, preheat the oven to 350°F (175°C, or gas mark 4). Line a baking sheet with parchment paper.

Add ½ tablespoon (8 ml) of the olive oil to a frying pan over medium-high heat. Add the onion and the mushrooms, and sauté for 3 to 4 minutes, until fragrant and soft. Transfer to a blender or a food processor with the white beans, tomato paste, salt, parsley, lemon juice and pepper. Blend until smooth.

Transfer the mixture to a large mixing bowl and combine it with the flour. It should be quite thick, but not dry. Dampen your hands slightly and shape the dough into 6 sausages, around 4 to 5 inches (10 to 13 cm) in length.

To fry: Add the remaining olive oil to a frying pan over medium-high heat. Fry 3 sausages for around 3 to 4 minutes per batch, until crispy and golden. Repeat with the remaining sausages, making sure not to overcrowd the pan.

To bake: Evenly space the sausages on the baking sheet and bake in the preheated oven for 12 to 15 minutes, until crispy on the outside and golden brown.

Lemon Poppyseed Pancakes with Chia Jam

MAKES 7 TO 8 PANCAKES

PANCAKES

¾ cup (90 g) gluten-free oat flour

1½ tbsp (14 g) poppy seeds

½ tsp baking powder

1 tsp baking soda

½ tsp ground turmeric

¾ cup (180 ml) plant-based milk

2 tbsp (30 ml) maple syrup

1 tbsp (15 ml) lemon juice

½ tsp vanilla extract

Olive oil, for cooking

CHIA JAM

½ cup (62 g) fresh raspberries

1 tbsp (15 ml) maple syrup

1½ tbsp (23 ml) lemon juice

1½ tbsp (15 g) chia seeds

TOPPINGS

Nut butter of your choice

Desiccated coconut

Chopped dark chocolate

Fluffy, sweet pancakes served with a cup of your favorite tea or coffee can make an ordinary weekend morning at home feel extra special. And a homemade jam always tastes extra luxurious, especially when served fresh and still warm!

To make the pancakes: In a large mixing bowl, combine the oat flour, poppy seeds, baking powder, baking soda, turmeric, plant-based milk, maple syrup, lemon juice and vanilla. Whisk together until no lumps remain.

Grease a nonstick frying pan with a little olive oil. Transfer around 2 to 3 tablespoons (30 to 45 ml) of batter per pancake to the frying pan and cook for around 2 minutes over medium heat, until crispy around the edges. Flip and cook for 1 minute on the other side.

To make the chia jam: Add the raspberries, maple syrup and lemon juice to a saucepan. Stir everything together over medium heat, pressing on the berries with a spoon to break them down. Once a compote-like consistency is formed, usually after around 2 to 3 minutes, stir in the chia seeds.

Transfer the jam to a small bowl and allow it to cool for around 5 minutes before stirring and serving with the pancakes. Serve with the suggested toppings, or switch them up if you'd prefer.

NOTE: Store any leftover jam in an airtight jar for up to 4 to 5 days. Serve it with a variety of dishes: how about adding it to Strawberry Birthday Cake Dessert Pizza (page 123)?

Turmeric Banana Mylkshake

MAKES 1 SERVING

MYLKSHAKE

1 medium ripe banana (preferably frozen)

½ cup (120 ml) canned full-fat coconut milk

1 tsp ground turmeric

1 tbsp (15 ml) maple syrup

¼ cup (23 g) oats

½ cup (120 ml) plant-based milk

TOPPINGS

Nut butter of your choice

Desiccated coconut

Pomegranate seeds

Shaved vegan chocolate

Served in a glass or a bowl with a variety of toppings, this mylkshake is sure to energize your morning and keep you satisfied until lunch. Serve it with the fruit of your choice, granola and a drizzle of nut butter or tahini to take this breakfast to the next level. For extra creaminess, freeze your bananas overnight.

Add the banana, coconut milk, turmeric, maple syrup, oats and plant-based milk to a blender or food processor. Blend until smooth.

Serve with the suggested toppings, or switch them up if you'd prefer.

NOTE: Add less milk for an even thicker consistency.

Chickpea Egg Muffins

MAKES 12 MUFFINS

- 1 cup (92 g) chickpea flour
- ¼ cup (32 g) nutritional yeast
- 1 tsp ground cumin
- 1 tsp ground turmeric
- ½ tsp garlic granules or garlic powder
- ½ tsp black salt (optional; creates an eggy flavor, but sea salt can be used instead)
- ½ tsp black pepper
- ¼ tsp baking powder
- 1¼ cups (300 ml) plant-based milk
- 1 tbsp (15 ml) lemon juice
- 1 tsp olive oil
- ½ (15-oz [425-g]) can chickpeas
- ½ medium onion, chopped
- ¼ large red bell pepper, chopped
- ¼ cup (16 g) chopped fresh dill

Eggs and egg-based dishes may seem difficult to veganize, but these egg muffins are practically effortless and need no fancy ingredients. Chickpea flour is a great way to create an eggy flavor, while the nutritional yeast brings in a cheesy undertone. Serve these on their own or with a dipping sauce of your choice as a quick bite on the go, or as part of a delicious brunch buffet.

Preheat the oven to 350°F (175°C, or gas mark 4). Line a 12-cup muffin tin with cupcake liners.

In a large mixing bowl, whisk together the chickpea flour, nutritional yeast, cumin, turmeric, garlic granules, salt, pepper, baking powder, plant-based milk, lemon juice and olive oil.

In a separate bowl, roughly mash the chickpeas, leaving around half of them whole. Add the chickpeas to the batter along with the onion, bell pepper and dill. Stir well.

Divide the batter between the 12 cupcake liners, filling each one around halfway. Bake in the preheated oven for 12 to 15 minutes, until fully cooked through but not dried out. They should still be a little bit soft on the inside to replicate an eggy texture.

Flourless Raspberry Banana Bread

MAKES 10 TO 12 SERVINGS

1 cup (104 g) almond flour

1 cup (100 g) coconut flour

1 tsp baking powder

1 tsp baking soda

¼ tsp salt

2½ large bananas, mashed

⅓ cup (80 ml) melted coconut oil

½ cup (120 ml) maple syrup

¼ cup plus 3 tbsp (72 g) ground flaxseed

1 tsp vanilla extract

⅔ cup (80 g) frozen raspberries (plus more for decorating)

As far as moist banana breads go, this one takes the prize. Seriously, whenever I make this, it's gone in under 24 hours—and I live alone, so I'm not sure whether I should be proud or concerned! Regardless, a slice of this bread is perfect with a thick layer of peanut butter and your favorite warm beverage, as the most indulgent dessert for breakfast. Plus, in terms of time, all you need is 35 minutes!

Preheat the oven to 350°F (175°C, or gas mark 4). Line a 9 x 4–inch (23 x 10–cm) loaf pan with parchment paper.

Add the almond flour, coconut flour, baking powder, baking soda and salt to a large mixing bowl. Stir well. Add the mashed bananas, coconut oil, maple syrup, flaxseed and vanilla. Mix to form the batter, then fold in the frozen raspberries.

Pour the batter into the loaf pan and cover it with aluminum foil. Bake in the preheated oven for 25 to 30 minutes. Leave the bread to cool fully before slicing and decorate with more raspberries before serving.

Pea and Zucchini Fritters with Smashed Avocado

MAKES 6 FRITTERS

- 1 medium onion, chopped
- 2 cloves garlic, minced
- ½ cup (60 g) peeled and grated zucchini
- 1½ cups (225 g) grated potatoes
- 3 tbsp (18 g) chickpea flour
- 1 tsp ground cumin
- 1 tsp ground turmeric
- 2 tbsp (30 ml) tamari
- 1 tbsp (15 ml) lemon juice
- ½ cup (67 g) green peas
- Olive oil, for frying
- 1 large avocado, pitted and peeled
- 2 tbsp (30 ml) apple cider vinegar
- ½ tsp salt, or to taste
- Black pepper
- Vegetables of your choice

My love for eating plenty of vegetables is endless, and fritters happen to be one of the most delicious ways to get in a couple of servings first thing in the morning. The texture is exactly how it needs to be: crispy on the outside, with a slightly chewy center. Add a smashed avocado sauce to balance out the earthy fritters with a milder flavor, and easily refrigerate or freeze any leftover fritters.

Add the onion, garlic, zucchini, potatoes, chickpea flour, cumin, turmeric, tamari, lemon juice and green peas to a large mixing bowl. Stir well.

Add olive oil to a large frying pan over medium heat. Use damp hands to form the mixture into palm-sized fritters, about 1 inch (2.5 cm) thick. Flatten each one down on the frying pan using a spatula and cook for 3 to 4 minutes. Flip and cook for 2 to 3 minutes, until crispy and golden.

In a small bowl, mash the avocado using a fork. Stir in the apple cider vinegar, salt and pepper.

Serve the fritters with the avocado sauce and any other vegetables of your choice.

Peanut Butter Baked Oatmeal

MAKES 2 SERVINGS

1 cup (90 g) gluten-free oats

2½ cups (600 ml) plant-based milk

2 tbsp (30 ml) maple syrup

2 tbsp (18 g) smooth peanut butter

¼ cup (27 g) chopped pecans

2 tbsp (30 ml) lemon juice

Baked oats are a healthy start to the day, and this version tastes like an indulgent dessert. Standard stovetop porridge is great, but baked oatmeal tastes like you're eating cake for breakfast despite being a wholesome meal that will fuel your morning. If I feel like adding an extra layer of decadence, I throw in a handful of dairy-free chocolate chips. You can also sprinkle with chopped nuts, shaved coconut or other toppings of your choice.

Preheat the oven to 400°F (200°C, or gas mark 6).

Combine the oats, plant-based milk, maple syrup, peanut butter, pecans and lemon juice in a large mixing bowl. Transfer the mixture to a medium-sized baking dish. I use a 9 x 4–inch (23 x 10–cm) dish. Bake in the preheated oven for 30 minutes, until golden and cooked through.

Tahini Chickpea Scramble on Sweet Potato Toast

MAKES 2 SERVINGS

1 tbsp (15 ml) olive oil

1 medium sweet potato, sliced into toasts

1 (15-oz [425-g]) can chickpeas, drained and rinsed

1 medium red onion, chopped

1 medium red bell pepper, chopped

1 clove garlic, minced

1 tbsp (15 g) tahini

½ tsp ground cumin

½ tsp ground turmeric

½ tsp curry powder

½ tsp salt

Black pepper

1 avocado, mashed (optional)

Want to switch up your usual scrambled tofu? Try scrambled chickpeas instead! This recipe shows off the power of natural, earthy flavors and the versatility of something as simple as chickpeas. The addition of tahini is not to be missed: it helps create a softer texture and enhances the flavor. Serve over sweet potato toast as a fun alternative to bread. Ordinary gluten-free bread, such as my Classic Seeded Loaf (page 127), works great, too. Your breakfast or brunch will feel luxurious, all from the comfort of your own kitchen.

Heat the olive oil in a large frying pan over medium-high heat. Lay out the sweet potato slices and cook for around 7 to 8 minutes. Flip and cook for 3 to 4 minutes, until golden and fully cooked through. Remove and set aside.

Meanwhile, add the chickpeas to a large mixing bowl. Mash them using a fork but leave some intact for a little texture. Combine them with the onion, bell pepper, garlic, tahini, cumin, turmeric, curry powder, salt and black pepper to taste.

Transfer the chickpea mixture to the frying pan and sauté over medium-high heat for around 3 to 4 minutes, until slightly crispy but not dried out. Serve over the sweet potato toasts with mashed avocado (if using).

Heathier Comfort Food Deluxe

Nothing says earthy to me more than rich, hearty and savory food that will impress anyone. Whether for a weeknight dinner or a dinner party where the appetites of a dozen people are at stake, I love getting creative in the kitchen and discovering new ways to combine my favorite ingredients. My blog started with savory recipes that helped people eat delicious, healthy food on a regular basis, so these recipes are close to my heart. They range from soups and pasta dishes to fusion cuisine and even a healthier alternative to the classic British roast dinner (page 44) to make sure you never have a boring lunch or dinner again.

Quinoa-Stuffed Eggplant with Whipped Tahini

MAKES 2 SERVINGS

EGGPLANT

2 medium eggplants
1 tsp olive oil
1 medium onion, chopped
2 cloves garlic, minced
1 tbsp (16 g) tomato paste
1 tsp paprika
1 tsp ground cumin
1 red bell pepper, chopped
¼ cup (43 g) quinoa
½ cup (120 ml) vegetable stock

WHIPPED TAHINI SAUCE

½ cup (120 g) tahini
1 clove garlic
Juice of ½ lemon
½ tsp salt

This stuffed eggplant is one of my favorite recipes. It reminds me of holidays to Greece where I always eat enormous amounts of eggplant—or aubergine, as it's called here in the U.K. They keep really well in the fridge in an airtight container, and they taste incredible with the mild whipped tahini sauce, which balances out the slight spiciness of the quinoa filling.

Preheat the oven to 350°F (175°C, or gas mark 4). Line a baking sheet with parchment paper.

To make the eggplant: Slice the eggplants in half, leaving the stems in place. Use a teaspoon to scoop out the flesh and set it aside. Lay out the eggplants on the lined baking sheet and bake for around 10 minutes.

Meanwhile, heat the olive oil in a frying pan over medium-high heat. Add the onion, garlic, tomato paste, paprika and cumin. Sauté for 3 to 4 minutes, until soft and fragrant. Add the bell pepper and the eggplant flesh. Stir everything together for 2 minutes.

Add the quinoa and vegetable stock. Simmer over medium heat for around 15 minutes, until the liquid is absorbed and the quinoa is softening. Add more vegetable stock if it starts to dry out too quickly.

Remove the eggplants from the oven and fill each eggplant half with a quarter of the filling. Place back in the oven and bake for 15 minutes.

To make the whipped tahini sauce: Place the tahini, garlic, lemon juice and salt into a blender or food processor. Blend on a low speed and gradually pour in water 2 tablespoons (30 ml) at a time, up to ½ cup (120 ml). Add more if you want a thinner sauce.

Lentil Shepherd's Pie

MAKES 6 SERVINGS

- 3–4 medium white potatoes, peeled and chopped (around 1 lb [454 g])
- 1 tbsp (15 ml) olive oil
- 1 medium onion, chopped finely
- 2 cloves garlic, minced
- 1 tbsp (16 g) tomato paste
- 1 tsp ground cumin
- 1 tsp ground turmeric
- 1 tsp paprika
- 1 large carrot, chopped
- 1 large red bell pepper, chopped
- 7 oz (198 g) mushrooms, chopped
- 1 cup (192 g) red lentils
- 2½ cups (600 ml) vegetable stock
- ½ tsp salt, or to taste
- 2 tbsp (18 g) all-purpose gluten-free flour
- ¼ cup (60 ml) unsweetened plant-based milk
- 2 tsp (10 g) vegan butter (plus more for greasing)

Lentil shepherd's pie is the ultimate crowd-pleasing classic that's ideal for feeding vegans and non-vegans alike. I've shared it with plenty of committed meat eaters who preferred the plant-based version to the original! Full of savory, earthy flavor, this dish is also made with healthy and wholesome ingredients that show off the power of plants at their best. Serve on its own or with a sauce of your choice, freezing any leftovers for up to a month.

Preheat the oven to 350°F (175°C, or gas mark 4).

Add the potatoes to a large saucepan and cover them with water. Bring to a low boil and cook for 15 to 20 minutes, until fork tender.

Meanwhile, heat the olive oil in a separate saucepan over medium-high heat. Add the onion, garlic, tomato paste, cumin, turmeric and paprika. Sauté for 3 to 4 minutes, until softened and fragrant. Add the carrot, bell pepper and mushrooms. Sauté for 3 minutes, allowing the vegetables to soften. Add the red lentils and pour in the vegetable stock. Cover and simmer for around 15 minutes, allowing the lentils to soften and most of the vegetable stock to absorb.

Season the filling with salt and stir in the flour to thicken it. Drain and rinse the potatoes once they are cooked, transferring them to a large mixing bowl. Mash with a potato masher, stirring in the plant-based milk and vegan butter.

Lightly grease an ovenproof dish with vegan butter. Transfer the filling to the dish followed by a layer of the mashed potatoes. Cover with aluminum foil and bake in the oven for 45 to 50 minutes, until golden brown and crispy on top.

Sunday Roast Dinner

MAKES 6 SERVINGS

ROAST VEGGIES

2 lbs (907 g) starchy potatoes

2 tbsp (30 ml) olive oil

2 tbsp (16 g) cornstarch

1 tsp ground cumin

1 tsp rosemary

2 large parsnips, peeled and chopped

2 large carrots, peeled and chopped

1 cup (88 g) Brussels sprouts, halved

Salt

LENTIL LOAF

1 cup (192 g) red lentils

2 tbsp (20 g) ground flaxseed

3 cups (210 g) finely chopped baby bella mushrooms

½ medium eggplant, chopped finely

1 tbsp (15 ml) olive oil

1 medium onion, chopped finely

1 large carrot, chopped finely

1 large red bell pepper, chopped finely

2 tbsp (32 g) tomato paste

½ tsp black pepper

3 cloves garlic, minced

1 small bunch fresh cilantro, chopped

1 tsp sea salt, or to taste

3 tbsp (8 g) buckwheat flour

As far as British classics are concerned, you can't get more comfort food than a Sunday roast! While this one isn't traditional given the absence of animal products, it's just as delicious and probably takes less time. It features a moist and flavorful lentil loaf, colorful roast veggies and an umami mushroom gravy. And, given the natural and wholesome ingredients used, the final result is on the healthier side, too! You can store any leftovers in airtight containers and enjoy them over the next few days. For instance, the lentil loaf makes a great sandwich filling.

Preheat the oven to 400°F (200°C, or gas mark 6). Line two baking sheets and a loaf pan with parchment paper.

Chop the potatoes and soak in cold water for 30 minutes. You can use this time to make the lentil loaf.

Cook the red lentils according to the instructions on the package; this usually takes 10 to 15 minutes. Make sure they are cooked through but not mushy. At the same time, make the flax egg: Combine the flaxseed with ¼ cup (60 ml) of water and leave to soak for 15 minutes.

Add the mushrooms and eggplant to a lined baking sheet and roast in the preheated oven for around 10 to 15 minutes. Meanwhile, add the oil and onion to a nonstick frying pan. Cook over medium heat for 2 to 3 minutes. Then, add the carrot, bell pepper, tomato paste and black pepper. Lower the heat and cook, stirring frequently, over low heat for around 10 minutes.

GRAVY

1 oz (28 g) dried porcini mushrooms

2 cups (480 ml) vegetable stock

2 tsp (10 ml) olive oil

1 medium onion, chopped

1 tsp onion granules or onion powder

3 tbsp (5 g) fresh rosemary leaves

¼ cup (37 g) all-purpose gluten-free flour

¼ cup (60 ml) plant-based milk

1 tsp gluten-free vegan mustard

2 tbsp (16 g) nutritional yeast

At this stage return to the potatoes. Drain and rinse them, then transfer them to a large mixing bowl and drizzle with the olive oil. Add the cornstarch, cumin and rosemary and mix everything together well. Transfer the potatoes to the lined baking sheet, making sure not to overcrowd. Bake in the preheated oven for 30 minutes, then take the baking sheet out carefully, flip the potatoes and add the parsnips, carrots and Brussels sprouts. Bake for 20 to 25 minutes.

When you put the potatoes in the oven, continue making the lentil loaf. When all the ingredients are ready, add them to a large mixing bowl with the garlic, cilantro and flax egg. Season with sea salt to taste. Wait a few minutes until the mixture has cooled down and stir in the buckwheat flour. Transfer the mixture to the lined loaf pan and roast in the oven for 35 to 40 minutes, watching the top to make sure it doesn't burn.

Make the gravy while the lentil loaf and the veggies are in the oven. Cover the mushrooms with the vegetable stock in a saucepan. Bring to a boil, cover, take off the heat and let stand while you prepare the other ingredients.

Heat the olive oil in a nonstick frying pan or saucepan. Add the onion and sauté over medium heat for around 3 minutes. Add the onion granules and fresh rosemary. Sauté for 2 minutes. Add the flour and the plant-based milk. Sauté for around 2 to 3 minutes, working continuously to ensure that the flour doesn't stick.

Pour in the mushroom–vegetable stock mixture. Add the mustard and the nutritional yeast. Bring to a simmer and stir over medium heat for around 2 minutes. Transfer to a blender or food processor and blend until your desired consistency is reached.

Serve everything as soon as possible, as a roast dinner is best when everything is straight out of the oven!

*See photo on page 148.

Spicy Baked Mac 'n' Cheese

MAKES 4 SERVINGS

3 cups (315 g) gluten-free macaroni pasta

1½ cups (219 g) cashews (boiled for 15 minutes if using a high-speed blender; soaked for 4+ hours if not)

½ cup plus 2 tbsp (150 ml) unsweetened almond milk

½ tbsp (8 ml) maple syrup

1 tbsp (15 ml) sriracha

1 red chile pepper, seeded and chopped

2 cloves garlic

½ tbsp (8 ml) vegan Worcestershire sauce

2 tbsp (30 ml) tamari

1 tsp paprika

Juice of ½ lemon

Chopped walnuts, for garnish (optional)

Vegan mac 'n' cheese is a dish that truly anyone can enjoy. I really mean that. With countless varieties to choose from, it's easy to find one that suits your dietary preferences. This is the earthy version of mac 'n' cheese, which uses the technique of blending cashews as a base while the hints of spice add a unique twist. Think the fancy restaurant version of mac 'n' cheese! It is, of course, delicious simply cooked on the stove, but the extra 20 minutes used for baking really do help to enhance the texture!

Preheat the oven to 350°F (175°C, or gas mark 4).

Cook the pasta according to the package instructions, but for 2 minutes less as it will continue to cook during the baking process.

Drain and rinse the cashews and transfer them to a blender or food processor. Add the almond milk, maple syrup, sriracha, chile, garlic, Worcestershire sauce, tamari, paprika and lemon juice. Blend until smooth and creamy and no chunks of cashews remain.

Drain and rinse the pasta and transfer to a mixing bowl with the sauce. Stir well before pouring it into a medium-sized baking dish. I use a 9 x 4-inch (23 x 10-cm) dish. Bake in the preheated oven for 15 to 20 minutes, until it's a light golden brown on top. Garnish with walnuts, if desired.

Buckwheat Pancakes with Miso Chickpeas

MAKES 2 SERVINGS (ABOUT 10 TO 12 PANCAKES)

PANCAKES

1 cup (120 g) buckwheat flour

½ tbsp (7 g) baking powder

1 tsp ground cumin

2 tbsp (16 g) nutritional yeast

1 cup (240 ml) unsweetened almond milk

1 tbsp (15 ml) apple cider vinegar

1 tsp olive oil or cooking spray

MISO CHICKPEAS

½ tbsp (8 ml) sesame oil

½ medium red onion, chopped

2 cloves garlic, minced

2 cups (140 g) oyster mushrooms, shredded

1 tbsp (15 ml) tamari

½ tbsp (9 g) brown rice miso paste

1½ tbsp (24 g) tomato paste

½ tbsp (8 g) tahini

2 tbsp (30 ml) rice vinegar

½ tbsp (4 g) cornstarch

1 (15-oz [425-g]) can chickpeas, drained and rinsed

One of the best things about adulthood is that I can eat pancakes for dinner, and no one is there to command otherwise. But when the pancakes in question are savory, healthy and served with hearty umami chickpeas, I feel a bit better about eating them for dinner. I love adding oyster mushrooms to the chickpeas because they add a great texture and pick up flavors really well, but you can replace them or add other vegetables of your choice.

To make the pancakes: In a large mixing bowl, whisk together the buckwheat flour, baking powder, cumin, nutritional yeast, almond milk and apple cider vinegar until no lumps remain.

Heat a nonstick frying pan greased with 1 teaspoon of olive oil over high heat. Alternatively, you can spray it with cooking spray. Pour out around 2 to 3 tablespoons (30 to 45 ml) of batter per pancake and cook for 2 to 2½ minutes, until crispy around the edges and bubbles start to form on the surface. Flip and cook for 30 seconds to 1 minute.

To make the miso chickpeas: Heat the sesame oil in another frying pan or saucepan over medium-high heat. Add the onion and the garlic. Sauté for 2 to 3 minutes, until softened and fragrant. Add the oyster mushrooms and cook for 5 minutes, until they begin to soften.

Meanwhile, stir together the tamari, miso paste, tomato paste, tahini and rice vinegar. In a separate bowl, make a cornstarch slurry by stirring together the cornstarch with 2 tablespoons (30 ml) of water.

Pour the sauce into the frying pan with the chickpeas and stir to combine. Add the cornstarch slurry and stir for 3 to 4 minutes, allowing the sauce to thicken before serving with the pancakes.

Chick'n and Shiitake Mushroom Pie

MAKES 6 TO 8 SERVINGS

CRUST

½ tbsp (5 g) ground flaxseed

¾ cup (120 g) rice flour (plus more for dusting)

¾ cup (180 ml) boiling water

¼ tsp salt

2 tbsp (28 g) vegan butter, divided

FILLING

1 tbsp (15 ml) olive oil

1 medium onion, chopped

2 cloves garlic, minced

3 cups (210 g) shiitake mushrooms

3 cups (300 g) cauliflower florets

1 tbsp (16 g) tomato paste

1 cup (240 ml) vegetable stock (plus more if needed)

1 cup (240 ml) unsweetened plant-based milk (plus more if needed)

1 tbsp (15 g) tahini

1 tbsp (7 g) ground cumin

¼ cup (32 g) nutritional yeast

¼ cup (30 g) buckwheat flour

½ cup (67 g) green peas

3 tbsp (45 ml) tamari

Juice of 1 lemon

1 large ripe plantain, sliced

Making an entirely gluten-free and vegan pie from scratch may seem intimidating at first, but by closely following the steps outlined here, you will end up with a masterpiece. The crust is flaky, buttery and light, while the filling is full-flavored and thick. Shiitake mushrooms add a meaty texture without the need to use meat alternatives.

Make the flax egg by combining the flaxseed with 1 tablespoon (15 ml) of water. Set aside for 15 minutes.

To make the crust: In a saucepan, combine the rice flour, boiling water and salt. Remove from the heat, and when the dough cools down, add the flax egg and 1 tablespoon (14 g) of butter.

Dust a flat work surface with rice flour and roll the dough out into a thin sheet. Spread with around 1 teaspoon of butter, then roll into a long sausage shape. Push the edges toward the center to form a dough ball. Cover with plastic wrap and leave in the fridge to chill for 45 minutes. Take the dough out of the fridge and repeat this process two more times (three times in total).

To make the filling: Heat the olive oil in a large saucepan over medium-high heat and add the onion, garlic, mushrooms and cauliflower. Cook the vegetables, stirring frequently, for around 6 to 7 minutes, until the cauliflower begins to soften, adding the tomato paste after around 2 minutes.

(Continued)

Chick'n and Shiitake Mushroom Pie (Continued)

Add the vegetable stock, plant-based milk, tahini, cumin and nutritional yeast. Simmer over medium heat for around 5 minutes. Stir in the buckwheat flour and cook for 5 minutes, stirring frequently, allowing the sauce to thicken. Stir in the green peas, tamari and lemon juice and cook for 3 to 4 minutes, stirring around once every minute. If it looks too dry, add extra plant-based milk or vegetable stock.

When you take the dough out of the fridge for the third time, roll it out into the shape and width of your pie dish. At the same time, preheat the oven to 350°F (175°C, or gas mark 4).

Transfer the filling from the saucepan into your pie dish and add a layer of the plantain on top. Place the crust on top of your pie dish carefully, pressing it down around the edges. Bake the pie in the preheated oven for around 30 minutes, until the crust is crispy and golden.

Tofu Tikka Masala with Cilantro Rice

MAKES 4 SERVINGS

TOFU TIKKA MASALA

- 1 (10-oz [283-g]) block extra-firm tofu, cubed
- ¼ cup (32 g) cornstarch
- 1½ tbsp (23 ml) olive oil
- 1 tbsp (5 g) garam masala
- 2 tbsp (14 g) paprika
- 1 tsp dried basil
- 1 tsp salt
- 1 tsp ground cumin
- ½ tsp ground turmeric
- 1 medium onion, chopped
- 3 cloves garlic, minced
- 2 tsp (4 g) cumin seeds
- 1 medium red bell pepper, chopped finely
- 5 tbsp (82 g) tomato paste
- 1 (14-oz [397-g]) can chopped tomatoes
- 1½ cups (360 ml) canned full-fat coconut milk
- 1 tbsp (15 ml) tamari
- 2 tsp (10 ml) maple syrup
- 1 tbsp (15 ml) apple cider vinegar
- Juice of ½ lemon

Tikka masala is a dish that's easy to veganize, and each bite is packed full of flavor, spiciness and comfort. The cilantro rice has a touch of creaminess and a perfectly fluffy texture, making this a perfect meal to feed and impress a crowd. The tofu is coated in cornstarch and fried to make it extra crispy and help it absorb the flavors of the sauce!

To make the tofu tikka masala: Add the tofu and the cornstarch to a ziplock bag and shake to coat the tofu cubes. Heat the olive oil in a large nonstick frying pan and fry the tofu cubes for 7 to 8 minutes, rotating frequently, until a light golden brown color. Remove and set aside.

While the tofu is cooking, prepare the spice mixture by stirring together the garam masala, paprika, dried basil, salt, cumin and turmeric.

Add the onion, garlic and cumin seeds to the frying pan. Sauté for 2 to 3 minutes, until the onion is softened and translucent. Add the bell pepper and tomato paste and continue to stir for 2 to 3 minutes to allow the pepper to start softening. Add the tomatoes, coconut milk, tamari, maple syrup, apple cider vinegar and the spice mix. Bring to a gentle simmer, then cover and cook for around 25 minutes, stirring occasionally.

(Continued)

Tofu Tikka Masala with Cilantro Rice (Continued)

CILANTRO RICE

1 tbsp (14 g) solid coconut oil

1 medium red onion, chopped

1½ cups (278 g) white Basmati rice

Zest of 1 lemon

½ cup (8 g) finely chopped fresh cilantro

To make the cilantro rice: Add the coconut oil and onion to a nonstick frying pan and cook for around 2 minutes to soften, then add the rice and stir for 2 to 3 minutes to brown it. Pour in 3 cups (720 ml) of water and add the lemon zest. Leave to cook undisturbed for 12 to 15 minutes, or until the rice is cooked through and the liquid is absorbed. During the last minute, stir in the cilantro.

Finish the curry by stirring in the lemon juice. Serve immediately with the rice.

NOTES: Add 1 teaspoon of cayenne pepper to the spice mix if you want a spicier end result.

The tikka masala is an excellent freezer-friendly food, so don't worry about cooking too big of a batch!

Honeyed No-Beef Burger

MAKES 4 BURGERS

BUNS

2 tbsp (20 g) ground flaxseed

1½ cups (360 ml) unsweetened almond milk

½ tsp salt

1 tbsp (15 g) sugar

1 tbsp (12 g) dry yeast

¼ cup (60 ml) olive oil

½ cup (60 g) gluten-free oat flour

½ cup (46 g) chickpea flour

1¾ cups (280 g) rice flour

1 tsp xanthan gum

1–2 tbsp (9–18 g) sesame seeds (optional)

VEGAN HONEY

⅓ cup (66 g) sugar

1 tbsp (15 ml) lemon juice

Here's your foolproof guide to making the best veggie burgers at home from scratch, including the buns! I love making this when I have friends coming over and there are non-vegans that I need to impress. I love it when people recognize just how delicious vegan food can be! The burgers are also freezer-friendly, ideal for meal prep and taste delicious either hot or cold. In the summer, bring them along to barbecues and outdoor gatherings so that no one feels left out, regardless of dietary preference. The spicy mayonnaise on page 131 works super well on these.

BURGER PATTIES

½ cup (50 g) dry textured vegetable protein (TVP)

1 (15-oz [425-g]) can red kidney beans, drained and rinsed

⅔ cup (150 g) cooked beets

¼ tsp ground cinnamon

¼ tsp paprika

¼ tsp garlic powder

¼ tsp salt

¼ tsp ground nutmeg

½ cup (46 g) chickpea flour

2 tbsp (30 ml) tamari

1 tbsp (15 ml) vegan honey

Vegetables and sauce of your choice

Preheat the oven to 350°F (175°C, or gas mark 4). Line two baking sheets with parchment paper.

To make the buns: Make the flax egg by stirring together the flaxseed with 5 tablespoons (75 ml) of water. Set aside for 5 minutes.

Bring the almond milk to a temperature of around 95°F (35°C) in a small saucepan over medium heat. Then, stir in the salt, sugar, dry yeast and olive oil. Set aside to activate for around 5 minutes.

Add the oat flour, chickpea flour, rice flour, xanthan gum and flax egg. Mix until a dough forms, but make sure not to overmix because this will prevent the buns from rising. Divide the dough into four equal pieces and shape them into buns. Arrange them on one of the sheets of parchment paper and sprinkle on top with sesame seeds (if using). Set aside to rise for around 15 minutes.

Use this time soak the TVP for the burgers in warm water for 10 minutes and to prepare the honey.

To make the honey: Add the sugar, lemon juice and 2 tablespoons (30 ml) of water to a saucepan. Wait for the sugar to dissolve, and then stir over low heat for around 10 minutes.

Bake the buns in the preheated oven for 15 to 20 minutes.

To make the burger patties: Drain the TVP and transfer it to a blender with the red kidney beans, beets, cinnamon, paprika, garlic powder, salt, nutmeg, chickpea flour, tamari and vegan honey. You can save the rest of the honey in an airtight container to use in other recipes.

Shape the mixture into four even-sized burger patties, using around ½-cup (120-g) scoop of the mixture per burger, and place them on the other lined baking sheet. Bake in the preheated oven for 12 to 15 minutes.

They are now ready to be served with the burger buns, veggies and a sauce of your choice.

*See photo on page 3.

One-Pot Garlic Tagliatelle

MAKES 2 SERVINGS

1 tsp coconut oil

1 medium red onion, chopped

2 cloves garlic, minced

1 tsp garlic powder

1 tsp ground cumin

½ tsp paprika

7 oz (198 g) gluten-free tagliatelle pasta

1 cup (240 ml) unsweetened almond milk

2 cups (480 ml) vegetable stock

2 tbsp (30 g) tahini

3 tbsp (24 g) nutritional yeast

Salt and black pepper

Gluten-free flour (if needed)

Fresh cilantro or garnish of your choice

If you've never tried one-pot pasta before, it's a simple, but genius technique that allows you to cook both your pasta and your favorite sauce in one pot. You save time, you save energy and you save the need to do extra washing up, too!

Heat the coconut oil in a nonstick saucepan over medium-high heat. Add the onion and garlic. Sauté for 2 to 3 minutes, until softened. Add the garlic powder, cumin and paprika. Cook for 3 minutes. Add the tagliatelle, almond milk and vegetable stock.

Bring to a simmer and cook for around 8 to 10 minutes, until the pasta is al dente, stirring occasionally. Add more liquid by the tablespoon (15 ml) if it starts to dry out, but make sure not to add too much at first in order for it to absorb and form a sauce.

Stir in the tahini and nutritional yeast. Season to taste with salt and pepper. Stir everything well. You may wish to add a couple of tablespoons (18 g) of gluten-free flour if the sauce is not thick enough. Serve with fresh cilantro or any garnish of your choice.

Tempeh Chili over Cauliflower Mash

MAKES 4 SERVINGS

Most people won't believe that the chili is vegan or that the creamy, smooth mash is made from cauliflower. Make sure to make extra of both because chances are, all your dinner guests will want to return for seconds!

CHILI

- 1 tbsp (15 ml) olive oil
- 1 medium onion, chopped
- 2 cloves garlic, minced
- 1 red chile pepper, seeded and chopped
- 10 oz (283 g) tempeh, chopped into bite-sized pieces
- ¼ cup (66 g) tomato paste
- 2 tbsp (14 g) paprika
- 1 tbsp (7 g) ground cumin
- 1 (15-oz [425-g]) can red kidney beans, drained and rinsed
- 2 (14-oz [397-g]) cans chopped tomatoes
- 1 cup (240 ml) vegetable stock (plus more if needed)
- 1 tbsp (15 ml) maple syrup
- 2 cups (134 g) chopped kale
- 1 oz (28 g) dark chocolate
- Juice of ½ lemon

CAULIFLOWER MASH

- 4 cups (400 g) cauliflower florets
- 2 tbsp (16 g) nutritional yeast
- 1 tsp garlic granules or garlic powder
- 1 tsp salt, or more to taste
- 2 tbsp (28 g) vegan butter

To make the chili: Heat the olive oil in a large frying pan or saucepan over medium-high heat. Add the onion, garlic and chile. Sauté for 4 to 5 minutes, until the onion is translucent. Add the tempeh, tomato paste, paprika and cumin. Cook and stir frequently for 5 minutes, until fragrant and the tempeh starts to soften. Add the kidney beans, tomatoes, vegetable stock and maple syrup. Cover and simmer for 40 to 45 minutes over medium-low heat, stirring frequently. Add more stock if it starts to dry out.

To make the cauliflower mash: Bring a large pot of lightly salted water to a simmer and add the cauliflower florets. Cook for around 10 minutes, until fully softened.

Drain and rinse the cauliflower and transfer it to a large mixing bowl. Blend using an immersion blender. Add the nutritional yeast, garlic granules, salt and vegan butter. Continue to blend for 30 seconds to combine the ingredients. Adjust the amount of salt depending on your preference.

When the chili is almost ready, stir in the kale and the dark chocolate. Cook until the chocolate melts and the kale wilts. During the last minute of cooking, stir in the lemon juice and serve over the cauliflower mash.

NOTE: Make sure to cook the chili for long enough. The longer it cooks, the more the flavors will develop.

Onigirazu (Tofu Sushi Sandwich)

MAKES 4 SANDWICHES

- 1 (10-oz [283-g]) block extra-firm tofu, cut into thin slabs
- 2 tbsp (30 ml) tamari
- 1 tsp hot sauce
- 2 tbsp (30 ml) rice vinegar
- 1½ cups (270 g) dry sushi rice
- 4 nori sheets
- ½ medium avocado, pitted, peeled and chopped
- ½ medium red bell pepper, chopped
- ½ medium orange bell pepper, chopped
- ¼ large cucumber, chopped
- 1 medium carrot, peeled and chopped

I have yet to meet someone who doesn't love sushi. It's such a fun food to make, and it's easy to veganize. But surprisingly, not too many people have tried onigirazu—or sushi sandwiches. This recipe is inspired by my 2018 trip to Japan, when I learned to make these and to this day, have onigirazu at least once a week. In addition to the tofu filling, feel free to add any other veggies of your choice.

Arrange the tofu slabs in a rectangular container. Stir together the tamari, hot sauce and rice vinegar. Pour the sauce over the tofu and leave to marinate for at least 30 minutes.

Cook the sushi rice according to the package instructions. Drain, then leave it to chill in the fridge for around 20 minutes.

Meanwhile, preheat the oven to 350°F (175°C, or gas mark 4). Line a baking sheet with parchment paper. Bake the tofu in the preheated oven on the lined baking sheet for around 20 to 25 minutes, until crispy and golden brown.

Place a sheet of nori on a rectangle of plastic wrap, with the edges of the nori at a 45-degree angle to the plastic wrap. Add a compact square of rice in the center using slightly damp hands, followed by the tofu and a selection of the other ingredients—avocado, red and orange bell peppers, cucumber and carrot. Finish with another layer of rice on top.

Fold the corners of the nori sheet toward the center, and then wrap the sandwich in the plastic wrap. Set aside for a few minutes and set something heavy on top. Carefully slice with a sharp knife before serving.

Creamy Dumpling and Butter Bean Stew

MAKES 3 SERVINGS

1 tsp olive oil

1 medium onion, chopped

2 cloves garlic, minced

½ red bell pepper, chopped

5 oz (142 g) green beans, chopped

5 oz (142 g) oyster mushrooms, shredded

1 cup (240 ml) canned coconut milk

2 cups (480 ml) vegetable stock

1 tsp ground cumin

1 tsp garlic granules or garlic powder

¾ cup (93 g) corn flour

1 tsp salt

1 (15-oz [425-g]) can butter beans, drained and rinsed

2 tbsp (30 ml) tamari

¼ cup (37 g) all-purpose gluten-free flour, or to taste

1 tbsp (15 ml) apple cider vinegar

This warming stew has an incredible amount of flavor, texture and richness. The soft and fluffy dumplings are a unique twist and practically melt in your mouth. They were inspired by a dumpling soup my grandma always made for me. Garnish the finished stew with a fresh herb of your choice, such as dill or basil, and you certainly will not be disappointed.

Heat the olive oil in a large nonstick saucepan over medium heat. Add the onion, garlic and bell pepper and cook for 3 to 4 minutes, until softened and fragrant. Add the green beans and oyster mushrooms. Sauté for 2 to 3 minutes, until the mushrooms begin to shrink and the green beans soften. Pour in the coconut milk and vegetable stock, followed by the cumin and garlic granules. Simmer uncovered for around 10 minutes, stirring occasionally.

Meanwhile, add the corn flour and salt to another nonstick saucepan and slowly add ½ cup (120 ml) of hot water, stirring over low heat for around 1 minute total to form a sticky dough. Transfer the dough to a lightly floured chopping board and roll into a thick rope. Slice the rope into 10 to 12 segments and roll each one into a roughly spherical shape.

Boil the dumplings in the saucepan you used to make the dough for 3 to 4 minutes, until they start to rise to the surface. Transfer into the other saucepan using a slotted spoon. Add the butter beans and tamari. Stir thoroughly. Then, continue to stir and gradually add the flour to allow the stew to thicken. Adjust the amount of flour according to your preferred thickness. Stir in the apple cider vinegar just before serving.

Ukha (Russian Fish Soup)

MAKES 4 SERVINGS

- 4 cups (960 ml) vegetable stock
- 1 cup (150 g) finely cubed potatoes
- 1½ cups (192 g) peeled and diced carrots
- ½ medium onion, chopped
- 2 nori sheets, cut into strips
- ¼ cup (16 g) chopped fresh dill
- 2 bay leaves
- 5 oz (142 g) firm tofu, cubed
- ½ tsp salt, or to taste
- Black pepper

Ukha is a popular Russian soup, made with different fish and typically served on special occasions. It's easy to make vegan, and you can even replicate a fish-like flavor using nori. Add in any other vegetables you have on hand, and replace the firm tofu with silken tofu if that's what you prefer. This soup is best served with a side of crusty bread!

Bring the vegetable stock to a simmer in a saucepan over medium heat. Add the potatoes, carrots, onion, nori strips, dill and bay leaves. Simmer for around 10 minutes, stirring occasionally. Discard the bay leaves and add the tofu, salt and pepper to taste. Simmer for around 5 minutes before serving.

Sweet Potato and Jackfruit Coconut Soup

MAKES 4 SERVINGS

1 tbsp (15 ml) olive oil

2 medium onions, chopped

2 (14-oz [397-g]) cans jackfruit in water

2 medium carrots, peeled and chopped

2 tsp (4 g) ground cumin

2 tbsp (32 g) tomato paste

2 large sweet potatoes (about 10 oz [283 g] each), chopped

2 cups (480 ml) vegetable stock (plus more if needed)

1 cup (240 ml) canned coconut milk

1 cup (180 g) canned chopped tomatoes

1 tsp paprika

1 cup (91 g) broccoli florets

1 tsp salt, or to taste

Black pepper

Mashed avocado

Fresh dill

Nothing beats a comforting soup, packed full of vegetables and flavor, on a chilly day. This is a weeknight dinner that the whole family will love. Adjust the amount of paprika you use depending on the level of spice you desire—and maybe even add a teaspoon or two of hot sauce. Serve with creamy mashed avocado and fresh dill to balance out the spice and take this soup to the next level!

Heat the olive oil in a large, nonstick saucepan over medium heat. Add the onions and sauté for 3 to 4 minutes, until soft and fragrant.

Finely shred the jackfruit pieces using a fork until they have a pulled pork texture. Add the jackfruit to the saucepan along with the carrots, cumin and tomato paste. Sauté for 5 to 7 minutes, allowing the jackfruit to brown slightly and the carrots to soften.

Add the sweet potatoes, vegetable stock, coconut milk, tomatoes and paprika. Bring to a simmer and allow to cook for 15 to 20 minutes, stirring occasionally, until the sweet potato pieces are soft. Pour in more vegetable stock if the soup starts to get too thick.

Add the broccoli, and season to taste with salt and pepper. Allow to simmer for 3 to 4 minutes, until the broccoli is cooked through.

Divide the soup between bowls. Serve with mashed avocado, dill and more pepper on top.

Wild Rice Salad with Mushroom Bacon

MAKES 3 TO 4 SERVINGS

1½ cups (240 g) dry wild rice
3 king oyster mushrooms
1 tsp sesame oil
1 tbsp (15 ml) tamari
1 tbsp (15 ml) maple syrup
1 tsp liquid smoke
2 tsp (5 g) paprika
1 medium carrot, peeled and chopped
½ large cucumber, chopped
1 cup (55 g) chopped iceberg lettuce
3 tbsp (45 g) tahini
Juice of 1 lime
½ tsp salt, or to taste
Black pepper
1 tbsp (9 g) sesame seeds (optional)

This recipe right here will prove that salads need to be neither cold nor boring. A salad done right bursts with flavor and leaves you satisfied for hours, not minutes. It's a question of having a solid, carby base, plenty of texture, a good dressing and a fun twist—such as the mushroom bacon in this case. The versatility of a rice salad makes it suitable for winter party tables and barbecues alike. If you don't have wild rice, any rice variety of your choice would make a great alternative!

Preheat the oven to 400°F (200°C, or gas mark 6). Line a baking sheet with parchment paper.

Cook the wild rice according to the package instructions; this usually takes around 25 minutes.

Thinly slice the king oyster mushrooms lengthwise and then slice each segment into quarters. Heat the oil in a nonstick frying pan over high heat and cook the mushrooms for 4 to 5 minutes, until they soften and shrink down.

Add the tamari, maple syrup, liquid smoke and paprika. Stir for 5 minutes, then transfer to the lined baking sheet. Bake in the preheated oven for around 5 to 7 minutes, until crispy.

Drain and rinse the rice and transfer it to a large mixing bowl with the carrot, cucumber and lettuce. Stir well. Add the tahini and lime juice, then stir once again. Season with the salt and pepper to taste.

Serve with sesame seeds (if using) and the mushroom bacon on top.

Crispy Tofu in a Sweet-and-Sour Sauce

MAKES 2 SERVINGS

1 (10-oz [283-g]) block extra-firm tofu, pressed if necessary and cut into triangles

2 tsp (10 ml) sesame oil

1 medium onion, chopped

1 clove garlic, minced

1 (1-inch [2.5-cm]) piece ginger, grated

1 medium carrot, peeled and chopped into matchsticks

3 tbsp (45 ml) tamari

2 tbsp (30 ml) maple syrup

2 tbsp (30 ml) rice vinegar

Juice of ½ lemon

1 tbsp (16 g) tomato paste

1 tbsp (8 g) cornstarch

2 tbsp (18 g) sesame seeds

Chopped scallions

There are many ways to turn plain, uninteresting tofu into a culinary masterpiece. My preferred method is rather simple, and it's ideal for those occasions when I want to get dinner on the table in under half an hour: fry or bake until crispy, then combine with a sauce of my choice. The sauce here is of an umami variety, which works well with the chewy, crispy tofu.

Preheat the oven to 400°F (200°C, or gas mark 6). Line a baking sheet with parchment paper. Arrange the tofu triangles on the lined baking sheet and bake for 12 to 15 minutes, until a light brown color.

Meanwhile, heat the sesame oil in a nonstick frying pan over medium-high heat. Add the onion, garlic, ginger and carrot, sautéing for 4 to 5 minutes, until the vegetables soften and the onion is translucent.

Make the sauce by stirring together the tamari, maple syrup, rice vinegar, lemon juice and tomato paste. In a separate bowl, whisk together ¼ cup (60 ml) of water and the cornstarch.

When the tofu is ready, pan fry it for 5 minutes, rotating each triangle frequently. Pour the sauce into the frying pan and stir well to coat all the tofu cubes. Allow to simmer lightly for 2 to 3 minutes, then pour in the cornstarch slurry and continue to stir until the sauce thickens.

During the last minute of cooking, stir in the sesame seeds, garnish with scallions and serve with a side of your choice.

NOTE: It's important to get as much water as possible out of the tofu. Depending on the brand you use, pressing may be necessary. You can also freeze it overnight to get a firmer and chewier texture.

Grilled Cheese with Quick Kimchi

MAKES 3 SANDWICHES

KIMCHI

1 Chinese cabbage, sliced into 2.5-inch (6-cm) strips

1 tbsp (18 g) salt

3 cloves garlic, minced

1 (½-inch [0.25-cm]) piece ginger, peeled and grated

1 tbsp (15 g) sugar

3 tbsp (45 ml) apple cider vinegar

2 tbsp (30 ml) tamari

2 medium carrots, peeled and grated

8 radishes, grated

4 scallions, chopped

GRILLED CHEESE

1¼ cups (149 g) cashews

1 medium carrot, peeled and chopped

⅓ cup (80 ml) unsweetened almond milk

⅓ cup (80 ml) canned coconut milk

⅓ cup (43 g) nutritional yeast

1 tsp salt

1 tbsp (8 g) cornstarch

2 tbsp (30 ml) olive oil

6 slices gluten-free bread

This is the perfect grilled cheese, veganized. The stretchy, flavorful cheese goes well with the salty kimchi and the crunchy, fluffy bread. Get ready for your kitchen to smell amazing as you pan fry these sandwiches! I love to serve these for dinner, but they're also ideal for breakfast and brunch parties too. Grilled cheese like this is very rich and therefore goes well with a light and fresh salad on the side.

To make the kimchi: Mix the cabbage with the salt and set aside for at least 1 hour. Meanwhile, stir together the garlic, ginger, sugar, apple cider vinegar and tamari in a small bowl.

You can use this time to prepare the cheese. First, boil the cashews and carrot for 15 minutes. Drain and rinse them, then transfer to a high-speed blender with the almond milk, coconut milk, nutritional yeast, ⅓ cup (80 ml) of water and salt. Blend until very smooth. Pour the sauce into a nonstick saucepan and add the cornstarch. Stir over medium heat for 2 minutes until the cheese thickens. Remove from the heat and set aside.

After 1 hour, stir together the cabbage with the carrots, radishes and scallions, then pour the apple cider vinegar mixture over the top.

To make the grilled cheese: Add the olive oil to a large nonstick frying pan over medium-high heat. On a plate, add a layer of the cheese sauce over a slice of bread, followed by 2 to 3 tablespoons (30 to 45 g) of the kimchi and another slice of bread. Once the pan is hot, add the sandwich and use a spatula to press it down. Flip after 3 to 4 minutes and cook for 3 to 4 minutes. Remove the sandwich from the frying pan, then slice in half. Repeat the steps with the remaining ingredients to make two more sandwiches.

Smoky Tempeh Pizza from Scratch

MAKES 1 LARGE PIZZA

PIZZA DOUGH

¼ cup (42 g) ground flaxseed

1¼ cups (300 ml) lukewarm oat milk, around 95°F (35°C)

½ tsp salt

1 tsp sugar

1 tbsp (12 g) dry yeast

3 tbsp (45 ml) olive oil

1¼ cups (150 g) buckwheat flour

1½ cups (240 g) rice flour

TEMPEH SAUCE

7 oz (198 g) tempeh, crumbled

2 tbsp (30 ml) tamari

½ tbsp (8 ml) maple syrup

1 tbsp (16 g) tomato paste

1 tsp paprika

1 tsp liquid smoke

Juice of ½ lemon

1 tsp olive oil

CHEESE

½ cup (120 ml) unsweetened almond milk, divided

2 tbsp (16 g) cornstarch

2 tbsp (16 g) nutritional yeast

1 tsp ground turmeric

1 tsp garlic granules or garlic powder

I love having pizza and a whole range of snacks if I have friends coming over for a movie night—sometimes I even get them to join in on the pizza making! This recipe is special because it feels fancy and rustic, while offering flavors that anyone can enjoy. Switch it up by adding other vegetables and dipping the crust into a sauce of your choice. To save time, you can use a store-bought pizza base.

Line a baking sheet with parchment paper. Steam the tempeh for 15 minutes by placing it in a steaming basket over a pot of lightly simmering water. This will soften it and get rid of a bitter flavor.

To make the dough: Stir together the flaxseed and ¼ cup (60 ml) of water. Set aside for 10 minutes to soak. Combine the oat milk, salt, sugar and dry yeast in a large mixing bowl. Set aside for 10 minutes to activate the yeast.

Add the olive oil, buckwheat flour, rice flour and flaxseed mixture to the yeast mixture. Stir well to combine, then transfer the dough to the lined baking sheet. Use your hands or a wooden spoon to spread it out into a circle. Leave the dough to rise for around 10 minutes. Preheat the oven to 350°F (175°C, or gas mark 4).

To make the tempeh sauce: Stir together the tempeh, tamari, maple syrup, tomato paste, paprika, liquid smoke, lemon juice and olive oil.

To make the cheese: Add 3 tablespoons (45 ml) of the almond milk and the cornstarch to a saucepan and whisk to combine. Continue gradually adding the remaining milk and waiting for it to thicken before adding more. During the last minute, stir in the nutritional yeast, turmeric and garlic granules. Take the cheese off of the heat and set aside.

TOPPINGS AND FOR SERVING

Zucchini

Mushrooms

Vegan cream cheese

Side salad or dipping sauce (optional)

Spread the tempeh sauce over the pizza base and top it with dollops of the vegan cheese before adding the zucchini and mushrooms. Bake in the preheated oven for 15 to 20 minutes, until fully cooked through and golden brown.

Top with vegan cream cheese and serve the pizza by itself or with a side salad and a dipping sauce of your choice.

NOTES: This makes a rather thick pizza crust. If you want a thinner crust, simply cut the ingredients in half and prepare as written.

You can use crumbled tofu instead of tempeh or even make this with mashed chickpeas.

Pesto-Stuffed Crispy Potato Cakes

MAKES 6 POTATO CAKES

POTATO DOUGH

1 lb (454 g) russet potatoes

1 tsp salt

2 tbsp (15 g) tapioca flour

PESTO FILLING

½ cup (15 g) spinach

⅓ cup (20 g) fresh parsley

2 cloves garlic, peeled

2 tbsp (30 ml) lemon juice

½ tsp salt

2 tbsp (30 ml) olive oil

¼ cup (34 g) macadamia nuts

FOR FRYING

2 tbsp (30 ml) olive oil

Pancakes for dinner? Yes please! These potato cakes are a healthier comfort food, given that they are made entirely from wholesome ingredients, including a generous serving of greens in the pesto! Freeze any leftovers or store them in the fridge to enjoy for breakfast the next morning.

To make the dough: Boil the potatoes with the skin on for around 30 to 35 minutes, or until cooked through. The cooking time will depend on the size of the potatoes.

To make the pesto: Add the spinach, parsley, garlic, lemon juice, salt, olive oil and macadamia nuts to a blender or food processor. Blend until smooth.

Drain and rinse the potatoes, peeling them once they cool down. Transfer to a large mixing bowl and mash using a potato masher. Then, add the salt and tapioca flour, and use your hands to form a dough.

Divide the dough into 12 evenly sized chunks, using around ¼ cup (60 g) of the batter for each one. Use your hands to flatten down each chunk, adding around 2 tablespoons (25 g) of the filling into the center and spreading it out using a spoon. Flatten down another dough chunk and place it on top, sealing around the edges.

Heat 2 tablespoons (30 ml) of olive oil in a frying pan. Cook the potato cakes for 7 to 8 minutes on each side, until crispy and lightly browned, making sure not to overcrowd the pan. Serve immediately on their own or with a side of your choice.

Sides and Nibbles

Have a party or gathering coming up? Want to impress vegan and non-vegans alike? There's no need for boring salads or panicking at the last minute over what to cook, because the dishes in this chapter will certainly do the trick. A lot of these recipes make excellent snacks for movie nights and other occasions, too. For instance, I love bringing the Cheese and Onion Tartlets (page 86) to picnics, and I serve my favorite gluten-free focaccia (page 89) as a side dish at dinner parties. If you're worried about what to bring to a barbecue, my Balsamic Pasta Salad (page 97) is perfect!

Herbed Potato and Zucchini Salad

MAKES 5 SERVINGS

2 lbs (907 g) potatoes, halved

½ tbsp (8 ml) olive oil

1 medium zucchini, sliced

2 large tomatoes, diced finely

1 medium red onion, chopped

½ cup (32 g) chopped fresh dill

⅓ cup (5 g) chopped fresh cilantro

6–7 radishes, sliced

¾ cup (180 ml) soy yogurt

½ tbsp (9 g) salt

Juice of 1 lemon

1 tbsp (15 ml) gluten-free vegan mustard

½ tbsp (8 ml) maple syrup

Black pepper

To me, few things scream summery gatherings with friends and family as much as potato salad. The flavors are fresh and vibrant, and the ingredients are light yet comforting. Plus the whole dish can be eaten either hot or cold. Even better, this recipe uses healthy ingredients and no vegan mayo: in other words, be sure to save some leftovers for lunch the next day!

Add the potatoes to a saucepan and boil for around 15 minutes, until fully cooked through.

Meanwhile, heat the olive oil in a nonstick frying pan. Once the pan is hot, add the zucchini slices and cook undisturbed for around 4 to 5 minutes. Flip, and cook on the other side for 2 minutes. Remove from the heat and set aside.

Add the potatoes to a large mixing bowl with the tomatoes, onion, dill, cilantro, radishes, soy yogurt, salt, lemon juice, mustard and maple syrup. Season to taste with pepper and stir well.

Serve immediately with the zucchini on top or chill in the fridge for 15 minutes.

NOTE: Go ahead and make this a day ahead of time, because potato salad tastes even better after standing in the fridge for a while.

Sweet-and-Sour Black Bean Chickpea Roll-Ups

MAKES 8 TO 10 ROLL-UPS

If you want a simple and creative party table addition, this finger food may be the perfect solution for you! I love making vegan omelets from chickpea flour, and these roll-ups follow a similar preparation method. Just make them a little bit smaller than you would an omelet to make them easier to eat with your hands. Pack them full of the sweet-and-sour black bean filling, refreshing soy yogurt and fresh veggies for best results. And, of course, avocado works incredibly well combined with black beans.

CHICKPEA ROLL-UPS

1 cup (92 g) chickpea flour
1 cup (240 ml) unsweetened almond milk
1 tsp garlic powder
½ tsp ground turmeric
½ tsp ground cumin
½ tsp salt
1 tbsp (8 g) nutritional yeast

BLACK BEAN FILLING

½ tbsp (8 ml) olive oil
1 medium red onion, chopped
1 (15-oz [425-g]) can black beans, drained and rinsed
2 tbsp (30 ml) tamari
1 tbsp (15 ml) maple syrup
1 tsp hot sauce (optional)
½ cup (67 g) green peas

EXTRAS

Mashed avocado
Soy yogurt
Chopped tomatoes
Chopped fresh cilantro

In a large mixing bowl, whisk together the chickpea flour, almond milk, garlic powder, turmeric, cumin, salt and nutritional yeast. Set aside for 10 minutes.

Meanwhile, make the black bean filling. In a frying pan or saucepan, heat the olive oil and add the onion. Cook for 2 to 3 minutes over medium-high heat, until translucent, then add the black beans, tamari, maple syrup, hot sauce (if using) and green peas. Cook, stirring frequently, for around 5 minutes, until the beans are soft and refried bean texture forms.

Grease a nonstick frying pan and pour in around ⅓ cup (80 ml) of batter per roll-up. Cook for around 3 minutes over medium-high heat, then flip and cook for 1 minute.

Set aside and add around 2 to 3 tablespoons (30 to 45 g) of the black bean filling to each roll-up, followed by mashed avocado, soy yogurt, chopped tomatoes and a little cilantro.

Cheese and Onion Tartlets

MAKES 6 TO 7 TARTLETS

CRUST

1 large baking apple, peeled and chopped into slices

1⅓ cups (140 g) almond flour

6 tbsp (60 g) ground flaxseed

¼ cup (30 g) buckwheat flour

1 tsp xanthan gum

¼ tsp salt

7 tbsp (100 g) solid coconut oil

1 cup (100 g) coconut flour

FILLING

1 tsp olive oil

1 medium red onion, chopped

½ red bell pepper, chopped finely

1 (10-oz [283-g]) block extra-firm tofu or firm tofu pressed for at least 30 minutes

2 cloves garlic

½ cup (120 ml) plant-based milk

2 tbsp (16 g) nutritional yeast

1 tsp ground cumin

1 tsp ground turmeric

1 tbsp (15 ml) tamari

¼ cup (23 g) chickpea flour

Black pepper

Chopped scallions, for garnish

Chopped walnuts, for garnish

This recipe teaches you how to re-create a cheese and onion flavor with no cheese at all, not even the vegan kind. Sounds like a mystical concept and a rarity, but it's surprisingly easy to achieve, even without cashews which often serve as a base for vegan cheeses. Eat these hot or cold—they are delicious either way. And they look pretty gourmet as well! Aside from the creamy tofu-based filling, I love the crust which is tasty enough by itself. It is buttery, with that distinctive subtly sweet aftertaste often found in bakery-style pastries. But this one is homemade and entirely gluten-free, achieving its qualities using a secret ingredient!

To make the crust: Add the apple slices to a microwave-safe dish. Microwave on full power for 5 to 7 minutes, until softened. Mash using a fork. Set aside around ½ cup (120 ml) of the purée to cool.

In a mixing bowl, combine the almond flour, flaxseed, buckwheat flour, xanthan gum and salt.

In a separate mixing bowl, lightly press down the coconut oil using a fork to get rid of any lumps (but don't melt it). Add the coconut flour and apple purée and stir them together. Combine everything in a single mixing bowl and mix using a spatula—avoid mixing with your hands—and leave to cool in the fridge for around 1 hour.

To make the filling: With 20 minutes to go, add the olive oil to a frying pan over medium-high heat. Sauté the onion and bell pepper for around 10 minutes over medium-low heat to allow the onion to start caramelizing.

Meanwhile, add the tofu, garlic, plant-based milk, nutritional yeast, cumin, turmeric and tamari to a blender or a food processor. Blend until smooth and no texture remains.

Pour the tofu mixture into the frying pan with the onion and bell pepper. Stir over medium-low heat for 4 to 5 minutes, gradually adding the chickpea flour around 1 tablespoon (6 g) at a time, until the sauce thickens. Transfer to a bowl and set aside.

After the dough for the crust has been cooling for 1 hour, preheat the oven to 350°F (175°C, or gas mark 4). Transfer the dough to a flat surface and roll out into a very thin sheet, around ⅙ inch (4 mm) in thickness.

Use the outside of a cup, a small bowl or a round cookie cutter to cut out circles. Press these down into a muffin tray and bake in the oven for 4 to 6 minutes, until golden brown. Add 2- to 3-tablespoon (30- to 45-g) scoops of the filling into each one. Serve immediately or leave to chill in the fridge for at least 20 minutes. Garnish with black pepper, scallions and walnuts, if using.

Olive and Rosemary Focaccia

MAKES 10 TO 12 SERVINGS

½ tsp sugar

1 tbsp (18 g) salt

1½ tbsp (18 g) dry yeast

3 tbsp (45 ml) olive oil

⅔ cup (60 g) chickpea flour

2¼ cups (360 g) rice flour

1 cup (54 g) sun-dried tomatoes (not packed in oil)

¼ cup (45 g) pitted black olives

¼ cup (45 g) pitted green olives

3–4 tbsp (10–13 g) dried rosemary

I've always loved focaccia, but recently it has become one of my go-to baking endeavors over weekends, and it's my favorite treat to bring to party tables. There's just so much room to get creative with it: with toppings, add-ins and serving suggestions. This version is a classic, starring a chewy, fluffy texture, earthy undertones of rosemary and an abundance of zingy olives as a topping. To serve this at dinner parties, I'd recommend making two batches because the first one will be gone in minutes! This focaccia is best served dipped in hummus or spread with vegan butter.

Warm 1⅓ cups (320 ml) of water to 86°F (30°C). Combine it with the sugar, salt and dry yeast. Allow the mixture to stand for around 5 minutes to activate the yeast.

Whisk in the olive oil, then add the chickpea flour and rice flour. Mix well, then fold in the sun-dried tomatoes before using your hands to shape it into a dough ball.

Line a baking sheet with parchment paper. Flatten down the dough ball and stretch it out into a roughly rectangular shape around 2 inches (5 cm) in depth. Cover with plastic wrap and leave to rise at room temperature for around 45 minutes. With around 20 minutes to go, preheat the oven to 350°F (175°C, or gas mark 4).

Uncover the dough and decorate with the olives. Sprinkle the rosemary over the top and bake in the preheated oven for 15 to 17 minutes, until soft, fluffy and golden.

Maple Baked Sweet Potato Wedges

MAKES 4 SERVINGS

¾ lb (340 g) sweet potatoes (around 1 large potato)

2 tbsp (30 ml) maple syrup

2 tbsp (30 ml) olive oil

3 tbsp (24 g) cornstarch

1 tsp paprika

Sea salt

Sweet potato wedges pretty much speak for themselves. They are an excellent healthy snack to share with friends, and they're also perfect for a side dish, appetizer or finger food to bring along to parties. Soft and fluffy on the inside and crunchy on the outside, they achieve a perfect balance between sweet and salty thanks to the maple syrup. Serve them with vegan mayonnaise, tahini, simple ketchup or just by themselves.

Preheat the oven to 400°F (200°C, or gas mark 6). Cut the sweet potatoes into thick wedges. You can peel them, but leaving the skin on results in extra crispiness and texture.

Transfer the wedges to a large mixing bowl and add the maple syrup and olive oil. Mix, then add the cornstarch and paprika; do not add the salt yet, as this will make the wedges soggy.

Transfer the wedges to a baking sheet and spread them out into a single layer, making sure not to overcrowd the pan. Bake the wedges in the preheated oven for around 35 minutes, until fully cooked through and crispy on the outside. Flip after around 20 minutes.

Season the potato wedges with salt to taste and serve.

Shaved Brussels Sprouts Salad with Tofu Ricotta

MAKES 4 SERVINGS

This refreshing, vibrant salad is full of nourishing goodness and, when served with tofu ricotta, will leave you feeling satisfied for ages. It's ideal for outdoor parties and as a side dish for any dinner when you want to show your guests just how amazing salad can be.

TOFU RICOTTA

1 (10-oz [283-g]) block extra-firm tofu

1 medium onion

3 cloves garlic

2 tbsp (30 ml) apple cider vinegar

1 tbsp (3 g) dried oregano

¼ cup (4 g) chopped fresh cilantro

½ tsp salt

SALAD

4 cups (352 g) Brussels sprouts, trimmed and thinly sliced

½ large cucumber, chopped

1 medium red onion, chopped

4 cups (120 g) spinach, sliced

2 tbsp (30 ml) olive oil

2 tbsp (30 ml) balsamic vinegar

1 tbsp (15 ml) gluten-free vegan mustard

1 tsp salt, or to taste

To make the tofu ricotta: Add the tofu, onion, garlic, apple cider vinegar, oregano, cilantro and salt to a blender or food processor. Blend until mostly creamy but leave some texture.

To make the salad: In a large mixing bowl, combine the Brussels sprouts, cucumber, onion and spinach. Then, add the olive oil, balsamic vinegar, mustard and salt. Toss to combine.

Serve the salad with the tofu ricotta on top.

Lemon Cauliflower Rice

MAKES 4 SERVINGS

1 head cauliflower

1 tbsp (14 g) solid coconut oil

2 cloves garlic, minced

Juice of 1 lemon

1 medium red onion, chopped

1 medium carrot, peeled and chopped

1 yellow bell pepper, chopped

½ tbsp (9 g) salt, or to taste

3–4 tbsp (3–4 g) chopped fresh cilantro

Who knew that cauliflower could turn into so many things, from pizza bases to smoothies and even an alternative to chicken wings? One of my favorite ways to make cauliflower taste great is turning it into rice, which is a lighter, low-carb alternative to ordinary rice. You can serve it either by itself as a salad or as a side dish for meals such as curry or chili. I love keeping a batch in the fridge, especially in the summer, when I often crave refreshing and vibrant meals.

Remove the leaves from the cauliflower and grate it using the large side of the grater. You can also rice the cauliflower using a food processor and a grater attachment. I would not recommend using a blender because the texture will be too fine.

Heat the coconut oil in a large nonstick frying pan and add the garlic. Sauté over high heat for 2 to 3 minutes, until fragrant. Lower the heat to medium and add the cauliflower to the frying pan. Cook for 3 to 4 minutes, stirring frequently. During the last minute, add the lemon juice.

Transfer the cauliflower to a large mixing bowl and combine with the onion, carrot, bell pepper and salt. Garnish with the cilantro and serve.

NOTE: If you want plain cauliflower rice, do not combine it with the vegetables at the end.

Balsamic Pasta Salad

MAKES 4 SERVINGS

1 (15-oz [425-g]) can chickpeas, drained and rinsed
1 tbsp (15 ml) maple syrup
¼ cup (60 ml) olive oil, divided
1 tsp smoked paprika
1 tsp ground cumin
1 tsp garlic powder
3 cups (about 300 g) gluten-free pasta of choice
2 medium tomatoes, chopped
⅓ large cucumber, chopped
½ cup (77 g) sweet corn
¼ cup (45 g) pitted green olives, halved
¼ cup (45 g) pitted black olives, halved
3 tbsp (45 ml) balsamic vinegar
3 tbsp (45 g) tahini
½ tsp salt, or to taste
½ tsp black pepper

This one is for the warmer months specifically, but it's great for whenever you're craving something fresh, packed full of vegetables and comforting, chewy pasta. Adding crispy chickpeas brings in extra texture and some plant-based protein. Use any gluten-free pasta of your choice, and customize this recipe with whatever veggies you have in the fridge!

Preheat the oven to 400°F (200°C, or gas mark 6). Line a baking sheet with parchment paper.

Add the chickpeas to a large mixing bowl and mix with the maple syrup, 1 tablespoon (15 ml) of olive oil, smoked paprika, cumin and garlic powder. Transfer the chickpeas to the lined baking sheet, spread them out into a single layer and bake them in the oven for 35 to 40 minutes, until crispy and golden.

Meanwhile, cook the pasta according to the package instructions until al dente. Drain and rinse. When the chickpeas are ready, transfer the pasta to a large mixing bowl. Add the chickpeas, tomatoes, cucumber, sweet corn, olives, balsamic vinegar, the rest of the olive oil and the tahini. Season with salt and pepper, then toss to combine.

Serve immediately or leave to chill in the fridge for 15 minutes.

Potato Croquettes

MAKES 10 TO 12 CROQUETTES

1⅓ lbs (560 g) potatoes
1 tbsp (15 ml) olive oil (plus more if frying)
1 medium onion, chopped finely
½ red bell pepper, chopped finely
3 tbsp (24 g) nutritional yeast
1 tsp salt
1 tbsp (14 g) vegan butter
5 tbsp (75 ml) unsweetened almond milk
¼ cup (31 g) corn flour
¼ cup (40 g) rice flour
1 tbsp (10 g) ground flaxseed
½ cup (32 g) chopped fresh dill
1 cup (115 g) gluten-free breadcrumbs (optional)

How about some crunchy, savory croquettes that are soft and fluffy on the inside and bursting with veggies and herbs? They always get a yes from me! You can bake or fry them depending on your preferred method—the end result will be phenomenal either way.

Boil the potatoes whole in a large saucepan for around 30 minutes, or until fully cooked through. This will depend on the size of the potatoes you use. Drain and rinse under cold water, and peel when cool enough to handle.

Meanwhile, heat the 1 tablespoon (15 ml) of olive oil in a frying pan over high heat. Add the onion and bell pepper, sautéing for 4 to 5 minutes, until softened and the onion is translucent. Add the nutritional yeast and salt, stir together and remove from the heat.

Add the potatoes to a large mixing bowl and mash using a potato masher. Then add the vegetables, vegan butter, almond milk, corn flour, rice flour, flaxseed and dill. Mix well and use your hands to roll the dough into evenly sized croquette shapes. Use around a ¼-cup (60-ml) scoop of dough for each croquette. Dip the croquettes in the breadcrumbs (if using) before baking/frying.

To fry: Cover the bottom of a nonstick frying pan with a thin layer of olive oil over medium-high heat. When the oil is hot, add the croquettes to the frying pan and cook each batch for around 5 minutes, rotating frequently, until crispy and golden around the edges.

To bake: Preheat the oven to 350°F (175°C, or gas mark 4). Line a baking sheet with parchment paper. Arrange the croquettes on the lined baking sheet and bake in the preheated oven for 12 to 15 minutes, until golden brown and crispy on the outside.

Lemon Edamame Soba Stir-Fry

MAKES 3 TO 4 SERVINGS

10 oz (283 g) gluten-free soba noodles

1 tbsp (15 ml) sesame oil

1 medium red onion, chopped

7 oz (198 g) oyster mushrooms, shredded

¾ cup (116 g) shelled edamame

2 tbsp (30 ml) tamari

2 tbsp (30 ml) rice vinegar

1 tbsp (9 g) coconut sugar

1 tsp sriracha (optional)

1 tbsp (15 ml) sweet chili sauce

Juice of 1 lemon

2 tsp (5 g) cornstarch

2 tbsp (18 g) sesame seeds

In just fifteen minutes, you can achieve the most incredible flavors using a handful of simple ingredients, with soba noodles serving as a wholesome, comforting base for this recipe. A soba noodle stir-fry works well as a main, but I often serve it as a light and refreshing side dish.

Cook the soba noodles according to the package instructions. Drain and rinse under cold water when done. Meanwhile, heat the sesame oil in a nonstick frying pan or wok over medium-high heat. Add the onion and cook for 2 to 3 minutes to soften. Add the oyster mushrooms and edamame. Continue to cook for 3 to 4 minutes, until the mushrooms shrink down.

Prepare the sauce by stirring together the tamari, rice vinegar, coconut sugar, sriracha (if using), sweet chili sauce and lemon juice. In a separate bowl, make a cornstarch slurry by mixing together 3 tablespoons (45 ml) of water and the cornstarch.

Pour the sauce into the frying pan or wok and stir to combine with the other ingredients. Add the noodles and the cornstarch slurry. Toss everything together, until the noodles are coated in the sauce and the sauce thickens.

During the last minute, add the sesame seeds. Serve immediately, or chill in the fridge for around 15 minutes before serving.

For the Sweet Tooth

As much as I love my savory comfort foods, I always want something sweet after dinner! I also believe that eating a healthy plant-based diet must involve balance, which is what this book is all about. My perfect evening, after all, consists of eating tofu with a side of cauliflower rice for dinner, and treating myself to a big slice of sweet potato pie afterwards—even better with a scoop of dairy-free ice cream.

This chapter will supply you with sweet treats you can make for any occasion, whether that's a birthday party or a Friday night family get-together to welcome the weekend in style. In fact, I used the Salted Tahini Chocolate Chip Cookies recipe (page 105) to make friends when I started university—good food really does bring people together and helps others overcome social awkwardness!

Salted Tahini Chocolate Chip Cookies

MAKES 10 COOKIES

- 1 tbsp (10 g) ground flaxseed
- 1½ cups (190 g) self-rising gluten-free flour
- ½ cup (72 g) coconut sugar
- 1 tsp baking powder
- ½ tsp salt
- ¼ cup (60 ml) plant-based milk
- 2 tbsp (30 g) tahini
- 1 tsp coconut oil, melted
- ½ tsp vanilla extract
- ¼ cup (60 ml) maple syrup
- ½ cup (87 g) vegan chocolate chips

The perfect sweet tooth cure? A chewy, dense cookie with just the right sweetness, enhanced by a touch of salt and an undertone of earthy tahini, bursting with chocolate chunks. Tahini is one of my favorite ingredients partly because it makes such a great addition to plenty of sweet recipes. Serve these tahini cookies as an afternoon snack with a cup of tea or bring them along to parties and gatherings to impress your friends. You can also replace the chocolate chips with raspberries for a lighter, summery version—or have both at the same time if you're undecided!

Preheat the oven to 350°F (175°C, or gas mark 4). Line a baking sheet with parchment paper.

Make the flax egg by combining the flaxseed with 2 tablespoons (30 ml) of water. Set aside for 10 minutes.

In a large mixing bowl, whisk together the flour, coconut sugar, baking powder and salt.

In a separate mixing bowl, stir together the plant-based milk, tahini, coconut oil, vanilla, maple syrup and flax egg.

Add the wet ingredients to the dry. Mix in the chocolate chips. Form the dough into 10 equal balls, pressing them down on the lined baking sheet. Bake in the preheated oven for 12 to 15 minutes, until crispy around the edges but still soft in the center.

Leave to cool for at least 5 minutes before serving.

Rich Espresso Chocolate Cake

MAKES 16 SERVINGS

CAKE

3 tbsp (30 g) ground flaxseed

2 cups (320 g) rice flour

1 cup (120 g) buckwheat flour

1½ cups (300 g) sugar

1⅓ cups (128 g) raw cacao powder

2 tsp (9 g) baking powder

1 tsp baking soda

1 tsp salt

2 tsp (6 g) xanthan gum

1½ cups (360 ml) unsweetened oat milk

1½ cups (360 ml) hot espresso

¼ cup (60 ml) apple cider vinegar

1 cup (240 ml) olive oil

1 tsp vanilla extract

FROSTING

⅓ cup (75 g) vegan butter

3½ cups (420 g) confectioners' sugar

2 tbsp (30 ml) cold espresso

1 tbsp (6 g) raw cacao powder

½ tsp vanilla extract

GLAZE

2 tbsp (12 g) raw cacao powder

3½ tbsp (49 g) unsalted vegan butter

¼ cup (50 g) sugar

1 tsp corn flour

Chocolate cake? Phenomenal. Espresso? My morning beverage of choice. Chocolate and espresso together? That gets a double yes from me. This dessert is everything you'd expect from an exceptional plant-based cake: rich, moist, fluffy, undetectably vegan and bursting with flavor in each spoonful. It looks very impressive, too. And you don't have to be an expert baker to pull it off and enjoy something a little bit more gourmet than a store-bought alternative. My biggest tip for this recipe is to not eat all the batter before it's able to make its way to the cake tins!

Preheat the oven to 350°F (175°C, or gas mark 4). Make the flax egg by combining the flaxseed and 6 tablespoons (90 ml) of water. Set aside to soak for 10 minutes.

To make the cake: In a large mixing bowl, combine the rice flour, buckwheat flour, sugar, cacao powder, baking powder, baking soda, salt and xanthan gum. In a separate mixing bowl, combine the oat milk, flax egg, espresso, apple cider vinegar, olive oil and vanilla.

Add the wet ingredients to the dry and combine using a hand-held electric mixer. Scrape down the sides of the bowl with a rubber spatula and stir once again to ensure everything is well incorporated.

Transfer the batter to three 9-inch (23-cm) cake tins and bake in the preheated oven for 20 minutes, until a toothpick comes out clean from the center. When done, leave to cool fully; this usually takes around 30 minutes at room temperature.

To make the frosting: Add the butter to a large mixing bowl and slowly add the sugar while mixing with a handheld mixer. When all of the sugar has been added and the frosting is light and fluffy, add the espresso, cacao powder and vanilla. Mix once more to combine.

Once the cake sponges are cool, assemble the cake. Spread a layer of icing around ⅓ inch (8 mm) in thickness on one of the sponges and place another sponge on top. Repeat, and finish by spreading a layer of the icing on top and down the sides of the cake.

To make the glaze: Add the cacao powder, vegan butter, sugar, corn flour and 5 tablespoons (75 ml) of water to a saucepan over medium heat. Whisk continuously until all the sugar is dissolved. Pour the glaze on top of the cake or around the edges before adding any other decorations of your choice.

*See photo on page 102.

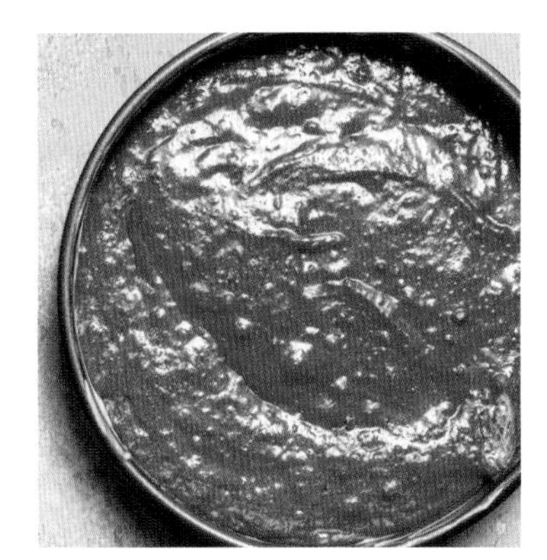

Raspberry Truffles from Scratch

MAKES 16 TRUFFLES

½ cup (62 g) fresh raspberries

½ cup (10 g) freeze-dried raspberries

½ tsp salt

⅔ cup (75 g) coconut flour

½ cup (112 g) coconut butter

½ cup (48 g) raw cacao powder

2 tbsp (30 ml) maple syrup

½ tsp vanilla extract

You just can't go wrong with raspberries and chocolate—and these homemade truffles will make you fall in love with the combination even more. They're made entirely from scratch, including the chocolate, resulting in a tangy, fruity center and a delightful crunch of a rich, chocolatey core. Truffles are a fantastic homemade gift—decorate with some icing and shaved coconut to brighten anyone's day on a special occasion!

Line a baking sheet with parchment paper.

Add the fresh raspberries and 1 tablespoon (15 ml) of water to a blender or food processor and blend for a few seconds. Then, pass through a fine-mesh strainer into a mixing bowl to get rid of the seeds.

Add the freeze-dried raspberries to the blender and blend into a powder. Then, add the salt, coconut flour and seedless raspberry purée and blend once again to combine.

Using either your hands or an ice cream scoop, shape the truffles. Arrange the truffles on the lined baking sheet and leave them in the fridge while you prepare the chocolate.

To prepare the chocolate: Melt the coconut butter in a small saucepan over medium-low heat. Remove from the heat, and add the cacao powder, maple syrup and vanilla. Return to the stove, and whisk together for around 1 minute, but be careful not to leave it on the heat for too long as the chocolate will get too thick.

Dip the bottom of each truffle in the chocolate, then place it on a fork and drizzle the rest of it using a spoon. Return the truffle to the parchment paper and repeat with the rest of the truffles. Leave in the freezer for 30 minutes, or in the fridge for 2 hours to set before serving.

Almond Honeycomb Bars

MAKES 16 BARS

BASE

1⅓ cups (127 g) ground almonds

⅓ cup (40 g) gluten-free oat flour

⅓ cup (53 g) rice flour

¼ tsp salt

¼ tsp baking soda

4 tbsp (55 g) vegan butter

1 tbsp (15 ml) maple syrup

HONEYCOMB LAYER

½ cup (100 g) sugar

¼ cup (60 ml) golden syrup

1½ tsp (7 g) baking soda

CHOCOLATE FROSTING

3.5 oz (100 g) vegan chocolate

¼ cup (50 g) sugar

¼ cup (24 g) raw cacao powder

6 tbsp (90 ml) soy creamer

1 tbsp (14 g) vegan butter

These taste better than any store-bought sweet I remember. The honeycomb layer is sticky and incredibly sweet, contrasting perfectly with a slightly crunchy base and a smooth, silky chocolate frosting. Just like the raspberry truffles (page 108), these make a perfect gift for anyone, in particular vegans who aren't sure how to re-create honey-containing favorites.

Preheat the oven to 350°F (175°C, or gas mark 4). Line a baking sheet with parchment paper.

To make the base: In a large mixing bowl, combine the ground almonds, oat flour, rice flour, salt and baking soda. Mix well, then add the vegan butter and maple syrup. Continue to mix until the dough sticks together. Transfer to the lined baking sheet and bake in the preheated oven for 5 to 7 minutes. Remove from the oven and set aside to cool.

To make the honeycomb layer: Add the sugar and golden syrup to a saucepan over medium-low heat and stir until the sugar dissolves. Remove from the heat and immediately add the baking soda, stirring vigorously until the mixture starts to foam. Then, pour over the almond base and set aside.

To make the chocolate frosting: Melt the chocolate by placing it in a heatproof bowl over a saucepan of water over low-medium heat, making sure that the bottom of the bowl does not touch the water. When the chocolate melts, remove the water from the bowl and add the chocolate along with the sugar, cacao powder, soy creamer and vegan butter. Stir together until the sugar melts and all the ingredients are well combined.

Pour the chocolate frosting over the honeycomb layer and leave to chill in the fridge for around 1 hour before serving.

Salted Caramel Sweet Potato Pie

MAKES ONE 10-INCH (25-CM) PIE

CRUST

2 tbsp (20 g) ground flaxseed

1 cup (160 g) rice flour (plus more for dusting)

½ cup plus 2 tbsp (75 g) tapioca flour

2 tbsp (15 g) buckwheat flour

¾ cup (145 g) muscovado sugar

¼ cup (55 g) coconut oil at room temperature

FILLING

2⅕ lbs (1 kg) sweet potatoes

½ cup (120 ml) soy cream

⅔ cup (160 ml) maple syrup

½ cup (60 g) tapioca flour

1 tsp vanilla extract

½ tsp salt

½ tsp ground cinnamon

¼ tsp ground nutmeg

CARAMEL SAUCE

½ cup (120 ml) canned full-fat coconut milk

½ cup (110 g) muscovado sugar

½ tsp sea salt

Sliced strawberries, for garnish

I am crazy about salted caramel: the contrast, the distinctive edge given to decadent sweetness by a subtle undertone of sea salt. If you can relate, give this recipe a go. Set aside a slow weekend afternoon to savor the baking process—and eat the sweet potato filling straight from the bowl. Then serve the finished pie as a centerpiece everyone looks forward to. This one will make your kitchen smell unforgettable! Make sure to use good-quality sea salt to get the most out of the recipe, and consider serving with a scoop of your favorite dairy-free ice cream while the pie is still warm.

Preheat the oven to 350°F (175°C, or gas mark 4). Bake the sweet potatoes in the oven for 50 minutes to 1 hour, until fork tender and caramelized. The exact time will depend on the size of the sweet potatoes.

To make the crust: First make the flax egg by soaking the flaxseed in 3 tablespoons (45 ml) of water for 15 minutes. Set it aside.

Lightly grease a 10-inch (25-cm) tart pan. Add the rice flour, tapioca flour, buckwheat flour, sugar and coconut oil to a large mixing bowl. Stir together using a spoon or a spatula, but don't use your hands to make sure the coconut oil doesn't melt. Once combined, mix in the flax egg.

Transfer the dough to a large surface lightly dusted with rice flour. Roll out into a thin disk, then transfer to the tart pan, pressing the bottom and the sides down firmly. Prick the bottom of the pie with a fork and add pie weights (e.g., beans, lentils or rice) over a sheet of parchment paper. Bake in the preheated oven for 10 minutes.

To make the filling: When ready, peel the sweet potatoes and mash them to make up around 3¼ cups (829 g) sweet potato purée. Combine the sweet potato purée with the soy cream, maple syrup, tapioca flour, vanilla, salt, cinnamon and nutmeg in a large mixing bowl. Blend using an immersion blender. Alternatively, blend everything together in a blender or a food processor on a low speed, making sure not to overdo it. Pour the filling into the crust and bake in the oven for 18 to 20 minutes, until crispy and golden brown.

To make the caramel sauce: Add the coconut milk, sugar and sea salt to a saucepan. Gently heat it up, stirring frequently, and bring to a simmer. Continue to stir for 1 minute until the sugar dissolves fully.

Serve the tart with the caramel sauce poured over the top and garnished with some sliced strawberries.

Double Chocolate Pecan Muffins

MAKES 7 TO 8 MUFFINS

MUFFINS

Coconut oil or cooking spray
3 tbsp (30 g) ground flaxseed
¾ cup (72 g) raw cacao powder
1¼ cups (200 g) rice flour
¾ cup (90 g) buckwheat flour
½ tsp baking soda
1 tsp baking powder
¼ tsp salt
1½ cups (300 g) sugar
3 tbsp (42 g) vegan butter, melted
5 tbsp (75 ml) olive oil
1 tsp vanilla extract
½ cup (120 ml) canned full-fat coconut milk
2 cups (480 ml) unsweetened plant-based milk
2 tbsp (30 ml) apple cider vinegar
¼ cup (44 g) vegan chocolate chips
¼ cup (27 g) finely chopped pecans

FROSTING

10 oz (283 g) dark chocolate
½ cup (120 ml) coconut cream
Shaved coconut, for garnish

In my opinion, the perfect muffin is tall and fluffy, sweet but not overly so, and with a finishing touch that makes it stand out from the crowd. This muffin recipe delivers on all accounts. You end up with the softest, most profoundly chocolatey muffins that will not last long in any household. No one will believe that the frosting is dairy-free and made with only two ingredients.

Preheat the oven to 350°F (175°C, or gas mark 4). Line a muffin tin with eight cupcake liners or grease the tin lightly with coconut oil or cooking spray.

Make the flax egg by combining the flaxseed and 6 tablespoons (90 ml) of water. Set aside for 20 minutes.

To make the muffins: Add the cacao powder, rice flour, buckwheat flour, baking soda, baking powder, salt and sugar to a large mixing bowl. Whisk together thoroughly.

Add the flax egg, vegan butter, olive oil, vanilla, coconut milk, plant-based milk and apple cider vinegar. Mix once again using a spatula. Fold in the chocolate chips and pecans. Divide the batter evenly between seven to eight muffin cups, filling around three-quarters of each muffin hole.

Bake in the preheated oven for around 20 minutes, until a toothpick comes out clean.

To make the frosting: Dissolve the chocolate and coconut cream in a saucepan, stirring until well combined.

Allow the muffins to cool down fully before spreading on the frosting, topping with some shredded coconut and serving.

Vanilla Cheesecake Bars

MAKES 9 BARS

BASE

⅔ cup (77 g) walnuts

1 cup (90 g) gluten-free oats

1 cup (178 g) dates

1 tbsp (15 ml) melted coconut oil

CHEESECAKE LAYER

2 cups (480 ml) soy cream, divided

2 cups (292 g) cashews (boiled for 15 minutes if using a high-speed blender; soaked for 4+ hours if not)

2 tbsp (18 g) agar-agar

1½ tbsp (23 ml) vanilla extract

Zest of 1 lemon

¼ cup (60 ml) maple syrup

I've tried numerous methods of making vegan cheesecake. Blending cashews achieves my favorite result: creamy and indulgent, yet with a distinctive lightness and just the right sweetness. The agar-agar helps the bars hold their shape well, which means you won't encounter any untimely melting. I recommend decorating them with fresh berries and bringing them along to a party table—or keeping them all to yourself and enjoying them throughout the week!

Line a rectangular or square dish with parchment paper. I used a 10 x 10-inch (25 x 25-cm) dish.

To make the base: Add the walnuts, oats, dates and coconut oil to a blender or food processor. Blend until well combined. It should form a sticky dough that holds together easily. Transfer the dough to the lined baking dish and flatten it down into an even layer.

To make the cheesecake layer: Add 1 cup (240 ml) of the soy cream to a blender or food processor with the cashews and blend until very smooth. Pour the other cup (240 ml) of soy cream into a saucepan over low-medium heat and add the agar-agar, stirring until it dissolves. Transfer the mixture to the blender/food processor with the vanilla, lemon zest and maple syrup. Blend once again to combine the ingredients.

Pour the cheesecake over the base. Decorate as desired and leave in the fridge for 2 to 3 hours to set before serving.

Key Lime Cashew Pudding

MAKES 4 SERVINGS

CHIA PUDDING LAYER

1 cup (240 ml) oat milk

1 tbsp (10 g) chia seeds

½ cup (75 g) mashed avocado

2 tbsp (30 ml) maple syrup

Zest and juice of 3 limes

1 tsp good-quality matcha powder

FROSTING

1 cup (146 g) cashews (if not using a high-speed blender, soak them for 4 hours before making this recipe)

3 tbsp (45 ml) melted coconut oil

3 tbsp (45 ml) maple syrup

2 tsp (4 g) good-quality matcha powder

Sometimes you want something sweet and indulgent without turning on the oven. I often find myself in this situation and making a no-bake pudding like this key lime treat is a solution that never fails me. Imagine a contrast between tanginess and sweetness, and a creamy texture paired with a delightfully green color. A smooth and light chia pudding layer is topped with cashew cream frosting for a treat you won't be able to get enough of!

To make the chia pudding layer: Whisk together the oat milk, chia seeds, mashed avocado, maple syrup, lime zest, lime juice and matcha. Leave in the fridge for at least 1 hour.

To make the frosting: If you have a high-speed blender and you don't need to soak your cashews, boil them for 15 minutes to soften them. Drain and rinse the cashews and transfer them to a blender with the coconut oil, maple syrup and matcha. Blend well until smooth and creamy.

Once the chia pudding layer is ready, divide between 4 jars and use a piping bag to squeeze the cashew frosting on top. Serve immediately.

Russian Napoleon Cake

MAKES 12 SERVINGS

DOUGH

2 tbsp (20 g) ground flaxseed

1 cup (120 g) buckwheat flour

1 cup plus 2 tbsp (104 g) chickpea flour

2 cups (320 g) rice flour (plus more for dusting)

1½ tbsp (14 g) xanthan gum

6 tbsp (75 g) sugar

7½ tbsp (107 g) unsalted vegan butter

CREAM

2 cups (480 ml) soy cream, divided

5 tbsp (40 g) cornstarch

⅔ cup (132 g) sugar

2 tsp (10 ml) vanilla extract

Growing up in Russia, my town was known for selling a whole range of cakes. Most, such as the well-known Napoleon cake, are packed full of dairy products and made with standard gluten-containing flour. It was a challenge to replicate the Napoleon cake while keeping it both vegan and gluten-free, but I love how it turned out: The cake is airy and light, soaking in the sweetness of the cream. The finished product practically melts in your mouth. Make this to impress anyone regardless of their dietary preference!

Make the flax egg by combining the flaxseed with ¼ cup (60 ml) of water. Set aside for 10 minutes.

To make the dough: In a large mixing bowl, combine the buckwheat flour, chickpea flour, 2 cups (320 g) of rice flour, xanthan gum and sugar. Add the butter and continue mixing, using a knife frequently to crumble up the mixture until you are left with a pea-sized crumb.

Mix in the flax egg before slowly adding ½ cup plus 2 tablespoons (150 ml) of cold water, mixing it into the dough using a rubber spatula. Do not use your hands as this may cause the butter in the dough to melt. Wrap the dough in plastic wrap and leave it to chill in the fridge for around 40 minutes.

Preheat the oven to 350°F (175°C, or gas mark 4). Line a baking sheet with parchment paper.

Remove the dough from the fridge and divide it into 12 evenly sized pieces. Place one of the dough pieces onto a lightly floured surface and roll it out into a thin sheet, around ¼ inch (6 mm) in thickness. Add more flour if the dough sticks to the rolling pin. Cut around the edges of the dough sheet to form a neat rectangular shape. Retain the excess dough as this will be used to decorate the cake at the end. Repeat the above process with the rest of the dough.

Lay four of the sheets on the lined baking sheet. Bake in the preheated oven for 5 to 7 minutes, until golden brown. Repeat with two more batches. When baking your final batch, crumble up any leftover dough and place it on the side of the baking sheet, but make sure it doesn't touch any of the dough sheets.

To make the cream: Combine ½ cup (120 ml) of soy cream with the cornstarch in a mixing bowl and whisk until no lumps remain. Then, transfer to a saucepan with the rest of the soy cream, the sugar and vanilla. Whisk while bringing to a simmer over medium-low heat and continue whisking until the cream thickens. Remove from the heat, transfer to a bowl and wait for the cream to cool to room temperature.

Apply a generous layer of the cream onto one of the cake layers and place the next one on top. Continue the process, finishing by applying a layer of the cream on top of the finished cake. Crumble up the dough scraps or, alternatively, you can put them through a blender or food processor. Sprinkle them on top of the cake, and around the edges. Leave the cake in the fridge overnight: this is really important as it will give the cream enough time to soak through the sponges. Slice into even-sized pieces to serve the next day.

Strawberry Birthday Cake Dessert Pizza

MAKES 8 SERVINGS

DOUGH

⅔ cup (160 ml) unsweetened almond milk

1½ tbsp (8 g) sugar

¼ tsp salt

1½ tbsp (18 g) dry yeast

3 tbsp (45 ml) olive oil

1 cup (120 g) soy flour

1 cup plus 1 tbsp (170 g) rice flour

SAUCE

1 cup (240 ml) soy cream

3 tbsp (45 ml) maple syrup

½ tsp vanilla extract

1½ tbsp (12 g) tapioca flour

STRAWBERRY JAM

1 cup (144 g) fresh strawberries, chopped

1 tbsp (9 g) coconut sugar

Juice of ½ lime

Pizza is great, but a sweet pizza is even better! Topped with a silky-smooth cream and strawberry jam, this dessert pizza is perfect for special occasions and for a sweet treat you can look forward to after dinner. You can add any other berries or fruit as a topping to customize it and make it even tastier! If you need any more persuading, this recipe takes only 35 minutes from start to finish.

Preheat the oven to 350°F (175°C, or gas mark 4). Line a baking sheet with parchment paper.

To make the dough: Warm the milk to around 86°F (30°C). Combine the milk with the sugar, salt and dry yeast. Set aside for 10 minutes to allow the yeast to activate.

Add the olive oil, soy flour and the rice flour. Mix well and knead using your hands to form a dough. Roll the dough out into a large flat circle and transfer to a lined baking sheet. Bake in the preheated oven for 15 to 20 minutes.

To make the sauce: Add the soy cream, maple syrup, vanilla and tapioca flour to a saucepan and whisk over medium heat until the cream thickens.

To make the strawberry jam: Add the strawberries, coconut sugar and lime juice to a saucepan. Heat up gently and stir until the strawberries begin to break down and a jam consistency forms. After around 5 minutes, remove from the heat and blend using an immersion blender.

Spread the sauce over the pizza, followed by the jam and any other toppings of your choice.

Vegan Basics with a Twist

The vegan community is known for its staple meals and anyone dabbling in plant-based cooking undoubtedly comes across them. And that makes complete sense: when changing your way of eating, you want to develop a bank of go-to recipes that never fail your taste buds. This chapter features many of my favorites ranging from bread (page 127) to homemade nut butter (page 135), but all with a bit of a twist.

Classic Seeded Loaf

MAKES 1 LARGE LOAF

1½ cups (360 ml) unsweetened plant-based milk

2 tsp (8 g) dry yeast

¼ cup (42 g) ground flaxseed

1¼ cups (150 g) buckwheat flour

1 cup (160 g) rice flour

1½ tbsp (14 g) xanthan gum

¼ cup (60 ml) maple syrup

¼ cup (60 ml) olive oil

¼ cup (35 g) pumpkin seeds

¼ cup (36 g) black sesame seeds

¼ cup (36 g) white sesame seeds

1½ tsp (9 g) salt

This is the only gluten-free vegan bread recipe you will ever need! Golden brown on the outside, soft and fluffy on the inside, this is a great weekend baking staple. Use it for sandwiches or serve it with your favorite nut butters—how about the Chai Spice Almond Butter on page 135? It is also great to dunk into cozy soups and stews. This bread is excellent for freezing! You can keep it in the freezer for up to 2 months and defrost as needed in the toaster.

In a saucepan, heat up the plant-based milk to around 86°F (30°C). Stir in the dry yeast and allow it to activate for 10 minutes.

Make the flax egg by combining the flaxseed with 5 tablespoons (75 ml) of warm water. Set aside for 10 minutes.

In a large mixing bowl, combine the buckwheat flour, rice flour and xanthan gum. Pour in the milk followed by the flax egg, maple syrup, olive oil, pumpkin seeds, black sesame seeds, white sesame seeds and salt. Mix the ingredients until a dough forms.

Transfer the dough to a loaf pan and allow it to rise, covered, for around 40 minutes. Meanwhile, preheat a conventional oven to 350°F (175°C, or gas mark 4).

Once the bread has risen, bake it in the preheated oven for 45 to 50 minutes, until golden brown. If the top of the bread starts to burn, cover it in aluminum foil and continue to bake. Allow to cool for 10 minutes, then cut into slices and serve with toppings of your choice.

Sweet Potato Dinner Rolls

MAKES 6 ROLLS

1 medium sweet potato, peeled and cubed

½ cup (120 ml) unsweetened plant-based milk

2½ tsp (10 g) dry yeast

¼ cup (60 ml) aquafaba (liquid from a can of chickpeas)

2 tbsp (30 ml) olive oil

1½ cups (180 g) buckwheat flour

1 tbsp (10 g) rice flour

1 tsp salt

Sesame seeds, for garnish

If you need something to take dinner to the next level, serve these sweet potato rolls on the side! Your family and friends won't believe that they are both vegan and completely gluten-free. These are best sliced in half and spread with vegan butter or topped with mashed avocado.

Preheat the oven to 400°F (200°C, or gas mark 6). Line a baking sheet with parchment paper.

Lay out the sweet potato cubes on the lined baking sheet and bake for around 40 minutes, until fork tender. Mash using a potato masher and set aside ¾ cup (191 g) of the purée (the rest can be stored for another use), then lower the oven temperature to 350°F (175°C, or gas mark 4).

Heat up the plant-based milk in a saucepan to 104°F (40°C). Stir in the dry yeast, then set aside for 5 to 7 minutes.

Add the milk, aquafaba and olive oil to a mixing bowl. Whisk together, then add the buckwheat flour, rice flour, the potato purée and salt. Stir together, until a dough forms.

Divide the dough into six even-sized balls. Lay them out on the lined baking sheet. Set aside to rise for around 20 minutes. Sprinkle with sesame seeds, then bake the buns in the preheated oven for around 15 minutes, until golden but still soft on the inside.

Spicy Garlic Mayonnaise

MAKES AROUND
2 CUPS (480 ML)

2 cups (292 g) raw cashews (if not using a high-speed blender, soak in warm water for at least 4 hours, ideally overnight)

2 cloves garlic

1 red chile pepper, seeded and chopped

1⅓ cups (320 ml) unsweetened almond milk

2 tbsp (16 g) nutritional yeast

1 tbsp (15 ml) hot sauce

1½ tsp (3 g) paprika

½ tbsp (9 g) sea salt

Juice of 1 lemon

This dairy-free, egg-free mayonnaise is what you bring to the table to make home cooking seem like restaurant-quality food. It pairs well as a dip with anything from chips to breadsticks, and it tastes delicious as a salad dressing when thinned out with a little bit of water. If you want a milder version, simply omit the chile and hot sauce, or reduce the amounts used.

If you are using a high-speed blender, boil the cashews for 15 minutes to soften them. Otherwise, drain and rinse the cashews and transfer them to a blender or a food processor. Add the garlic, chile, almond milk, nutritional yeast, hot sauce, paprika, sea salt and lemon juice. Blend until very smooth and no cashew lumps remain. Transfer to a jar or container of your choice. It can be stored in the fridge for up to 5 days.

Maple Walnut Butter

MAKES AROUND
2 CUPS (240 G)

2 cups (234 g) walnuts
2 tbsp (30 ml) maple syrup
½ tsp sea salt

Homemade nut butter is less expensive and much tastier than store-bought, and it's also fun to make and much easier than it seems! Walnut butter has an intense and earthy taste, especially combined with maple syrup and a pinch of salt. These three ingredients are all you need for a spread you won't be able to get enough of. Serve on toast, stirred into porridge or just by itself as a quick treat!

Preheat a conventional oven to 350°F (175°C, or gas mark 4). Line a baking sheet with parchment paper.

Spread the walnuts over the lined baking sheet and roast for around 10 minutes, until lightly browned, but make sure not to burn them.

Transfer the walnuts to a high-speed blender. Start on the lowest setting, then increase slowly to the highest and blend until it starts to get smooth and creamy. Pause to scrape down the sides as necessary. Be patient, as this can take up to 2 to 3 minutes. You can also use a food processor, but this will take longer to create a smooth, clump-free consistency—around 5 to 10 minutes, depending on the model.

Add the maple syrup and sea salt, blending for around 10 seconds to incorporate them. Transfer the maple walnut butter to a jar or container of your choice. It's best stored in the fridge for up to a week.

Chai Spice Almond Butter

MAKES AROUND
2 CUPS (435 G)

3 cups (429 g) almonds
2 tbsp (30 ml) olive oil
½ tsp salt
½ tsp allspice
½ tsp ground cinnamon
½ tsp ground cloves
½ tsp ground cardamom

There are countless nut butter combinations you can try—it's all about getting creative with add-ins and seeing how you can enhance the natural flavors of the nuts. This is an interesting twist on classic almond butter. It tastes delicious served on toast with banana slices or blended into smoothies to energize your morning.

Add the almonds and olive oil to a high-speed blender. Start on the lowest setting, then increase slowly to the highest and blend until smooth and creamy. Pause to scrape down the sides as necessary. Be patient, as this can take up to 2 to 3 minutes. You can also use a food processor, but this will take longer to create a smooth, clump-free consistency—around 5 to 10 minutes, depending on the model.

Add the salt, allspice, cinnamon, cloves and cardamom. Blend for 30 seconds to combine, then transfer to a jar or container of your choice. Store at room temperature for up to 2 weeks.

Spicy Baked Cashew Cheese

MAKES 16 SERVINGS

2 cups (292 g) cashews (if you do not have a high-speed blender, soak the cashews for 4 to 8 hours on the counter to soften them)

2 tbsp (16 g) nutritional yeast

1 tsp paprika

½ tsp ground cumin

2 cloves garlic

2 tbsp (30 g) tahini

2 tbsp (30 ml) lemon juice

When I first went vegan, the idea of making homemade cheese intimidated me. But trust me, the hardest part is probably waiting while it's in the oven: your kitchen will smell phenomenal! To make this for a party table, do the preparation the day before and bake on the day of the event. Then, proceed to impress everyone. Serve on crackers or as part of a creative vegan cheese board.

If using a high-speed blender, boil the cashews in a saucepan for 15 minutes.

Drain and rinse the cashews and transfer them to your blender or food processor. Add the nutritional yeast, paprika, cumin, garlic, tahini, lemon juice and ¼ cup (60 ml) of water. Blend well until completely smooth and creamy; no chunks of cashews should remain.

Transfer the mixture into a cheesecloth placed over a strainer and close the cheesecloth. Place the strainer over a bowl and leave it in the fridge overnight, or for around 8 hours. This will ensure that the excess liquid drains away from the cheese, which avoids a soggy texture.

The next day, preheat the oven to 340°F (170°C, or gas mark 4). Line a baking sheet with parchment paper.

Transfer the cheese to the lined baking sheet and bake in the preheated oven for 40 to 45 minutes, until golden brown. Serve immediately, or leave to cool for 15 to 20 minutes before serving.

Poppyseed Wraps from Scratch

MAKES 12 WRAPS

2 cups (320 g) brown rice flour

1⅓ cups (160 g) buckwheat flour

1 tbsp (12 g) dry yeast

4 tsp (12 g) xanthan gum

½ cup (75 g) poppy seeds

1 tsp sea salt

2 tbsp (30 ml) olive oil (plus more for frying)

These poppyseed wraps couldn't be any more versatile! Fill them with ingredients of your choice and take them with you in your lunch box. Use them to make veggie shawarma or kebabs or cut them up into triangles and serve them with a bowl of hummus. The possibilities are endless!

Add the rice flour, buckwheat flour, dry yeast, xanthan gum, poppy seeds and sea salt to a large mixing bowl. Whisk together thoroughly.

Pour in 1½ cups (360 ml) of water and the olive oil. Mix until a dough forms. Set aside and allow to stand for around 15 minutes.

Divide the dough into 12 evenly sized balls and grease a frying pan with olive oil. I recommend dividing the dough because rolling it out into a single sheet would require a very large work surface, given that the wraps are around 9 inches (23 cm) in diameter each.

Roll out a ball into a thin sheet about ¼ inch (6 mm) in thickness. Place a large bowl on top of the sheet and cut around the edge to form a neat circle. Transfer to the frying pan and allow to cook over medium-high heat for around 1½ minutes. Meanwhile, brush the other side with a little bit more olive oil. Flip and cook for around 30 seconds on the other side. Transfer to a plate and repeat with the rest of the balls. They are best stored in the fridge for up to 5 days, covered. They can be reheated either in the microwave, or over a lightly-greased pan.

NOTE: For a lighter version, don't use olive oil when cooking them in the frying pan, but remember they may be a little bit more dry in the end and won't roll up as easily if you want to use them for wraps.

Sliceable Herb Cheese

MAKES 10 SERVINGS

1½ cups (360 ml) canned full-fat coconut milk

2 tsp (6 g) agar-agar

1 tsp lime juice

1 tsp garlic powder

¼ cup (32 g) nutritional yeast

1 tbsp (8 g) tapioca starch

1 tsp salt

¼ cup (16 g) chopped fresh dill

On my quest to try various vegan cheeses, I pursued the idea of a cheese that's sliceable, melts in your mouth and is perfect for a light but decadent appetizer. I can also picture myself taking this one to a picnic or including it as part of a vegan charcuterie board with grapes, crackers and other fun snacks. Or, how about throwing it into Balsamic Pasta Salad (page 97)?

Add the coconut milk, agar-agar, lime juice, garlic powder, ¼ cup (60 ml) of lukewarm water, nutritional yeast, tapioca starch and salt to a saucepan. Stir over medium-low heat for around 5 minutes, until the agar-agar is fully dissolved. During the last minute, stir in the dill.

Transfer to a rectangular dish, such as a small loaf pan, and leave it to set in the fridge for at least 1 hour before serving.

Chocolate Oat Mylk

MAKES ABOUT 4 CUPS (960 ML)

1 cup (90 g) gluten-free oats
1 tbsp (15 ml) maple syrup
1 tbsp (6 g) raw cacao powder

There's no need for store-bought oat milk when homemade tastes so much better and is exceptionally easy to make. Enjoy this indulgent drink by itself, use it to cook oatmeal or serve it with cereal or granola for a perfect breakfast. Taste for sweetness and add extra maple syrup if you want more!

Add the oats, 4 cups (960 ml) of water, maple syrup and cacao powder to a high-speed blender and blend until smooth. Transfer the mylk to an airtight jar and keep it in the fridge for up to 5 days.

Optional: Strain the mylk using a nut milk bag, a clean t-shirt or a kitchen towel by stretching it over a large mixing bowl and pouring in the mylk.

PICKLED CABBAGE 3 WAYS

Fermented and pickled foods are delicious—and they're also good for you! I ate them a lot growing up and their wholesome simplicity exemplifies perfectly what an earthy food really is. Pickled cabbage requires minimal preparation, and the hardest part is waiting for it to be ready to eat. But once it is, it's super versatile and lasts for ages. How about adding some to pasta salad (page 97) or savory buckwheat pancakes (page 48)?

Quick Pickled Cabbage

MAKES AROUND 5 CUPS (750 G)

If you don't have a lot of time or simply don't want to wait for delicious pickled cabbage, this is the ideal recipe for you. Although ready in just half an hour, you certainly won't miss out on flavor!

- 1 medium head cabbage, sliced
- 1 medium green bell pepper, sliced
- 1 medium red bell pepper, sliced
- 1 medium red onion, chopped
- ½ cup (120 ml) olive oil
- 3 tbsp (23 g) sugar
- 1 tbsp (18 g) salt
- 6 tbsp (90 ml) vinegar

Add the cabbage, bell peppers, onion, ½ cup (120 ml) of warm water, olive oil, sugar, salt and vinegar to an airtight container. Stir well and set aside for half an hour.

Beetroot Pickled Cabbage

MAKES AROUND
5 CUPS (750 G)

1 medium head cabbage, sliced

1 large carrot, peeled and chopped

1 cup (225 g) chopped beets

½ red chile pepper, seeded and chopped

2 cloves garlic, minced

½ tsp black pepper

¼ cup (60 ml) vinegar

1½ tbsp (19 g) sugar

1 tbsp (18 g) salt

If you love bright and vibrant colors, this pickled cabbage is the one for you. And don't worry, it won't taste overwhelmingly like beets. Its inclusion simply adds a sweeter undertone and a beautiful pink color that will look—and taste—even better on avocado toast!

Add the cabbage, carrot, beets, chile, garlic, pepper, 1½ cups (360 ml) of hot water, vinegar, sugar and salt to a large container. Stir well and leave to marinate overnight.

Korean-Style Spicy Pickled Cabbage

MAKES AROUND 5 CUPS (750 G)

1 medium head cabbage, chopped

1 large carrot, peeled and chopped diagonally

1 red chile pepper, seeded and chopped

1 clove garlic, minced

¼ cup (50 g) sugar

⅓ cup (80 ml) olive oil

⅓ cup (80 ml) apple cider vinegar

½ tsp black pepper

½ tsp coriander seeds

1 tbsp (18 g) salt

I love spicy foods. That wasn't always the case: Once I had an extremely low spice tolerance, but now I love a kick of spice with most of my meals. Luckily, this pickled cabbage is great for putting on salads and pasta dishes to give them a unique twist.

Combine the cabbage, carrot and chile in a large mixing bowl and transfer to a jar or rectangular dish.

Add the garlic, 1½ cups (360 ml) of water, sugar, olive oil, apple cider vinegar, pepper, coriander seeds and salt to a saucepan. Stir over medium heat until the salt and sugar dissolve.

Pour into the container with the cabbage and let stand, covered, overnight before serving.

Acknowledgments

First and foremost, I want to thank my mum, Olga, for helping me develop and test the recipes in this book, for being my number one cheerleader through the highs and lows and for always being there for me. Furthermore, I couldn't thank my online community enough for their support and encouragement over the last couple of years—I definitely wouldn't be here without all of you! Last but not least, I want to thank my amazing publisher, Page Street, for giving me the opportunity to put my recipes out there and helping me throughout the process.

About The Author

Maria Gureeva is a vegan recipe developer, food photographer and entrepreneur. A few years after switching over to a vegan lifestyle for ethical and health reasons, she started her blog and Instagram page, Earth of Maria, which has grown into a community passionate about eating well and helping the world be a better place one meal at a time. She has been featured in print and digital publications such as *Thrive* and the feedfeed, and worked with well-known brands such as Sainsbury's, Whole Foods and Alpro. She studies history at the University of Oxford, loves learning and is a lifelong fitness enthusiast.

Index